WHEN GIRLS WIN

Mental Toughness Tips to Elevate Your Performance

MARYJO MCCLOSKEY

Dedicated to my amazing parents,
with enormous love and gratitude.

CONTENTS

WHEN GIRLS WIN

This is the story of
my journey in the arena—
the challenges,
the ups and downs,
highs and lows, wins and losses,
and mostly the self-awareness
and mental toughness tools that
I discovered along the way.
I hope my lessons guide you
on your own incredible journey.

Chase your dreams
and always remember to be
grateful and
fiercely authentic!

Cheers!
Coach MJ

1

I'VE GOT THE MUSIC IN ME

Even if it's not tennis, even if it's other dreams like in school and being a doctor or anything like that – dream big and anything can happen.

- Emma Raducanu, 2021 US Open Women's Tennis Champion

"Too many obstacles are stacked against you."

"No chance, no one can do it—don't even think about it!"

"Give up trying to compete for something that is impossible."

And the best one...

"There is no hope for a school located in wet and soggy Oregon."

All comments I heard 20-plus years ago when I first got into the business of coaching collegiate women's golf in Oregon. I was told by my fellow coaches that a golf team in our Conference would *never* be a national contender.

My retort? "Why not?"

And guess what? Our team from a small town in Oregon WON THE 2023 NCAA D-III WOMEN'S GOLF NATIONAL CHAMPIONSHIP! We are one of just three D-III women's golf teams west of the Mississippi to win a national NCAA Championship. Yep—we did it! We reached the top of the podium despite all the negativity and naysaying that it was an impossible goal! We dreamed the impossible dream and made it happen.

In fact, since I started this women's golf program as its very first coach, we have made thirteen straight visits to the NCAA D-III Women's Golf National Championship—and we most likely would have made 14, but the 2020 spring season was cancelled due to Covid-19. We have brought home *seven* NCAA team trophies including the 2023 National Championship, produced a National Champion, two National Runner Up Champions, have had two players named National Player of the Year, two players named Freshman National Player of the Year, and have been awarded 27 All Americans.

In other words, never say *never*.

I always believed that the impossible was possible. I always dreamed bigger—but over time, sometimes you wonder if you are chasing the wrong dream or going after something that you may not be capable of achieving even if you work really hard at it.

How did we reach the top of the mountain? It hasn't been an easy ascent. I had my share of setbacks, failures, and defeats on the way up. Sometimes I wanted to quit, but something inside me always pulled me back and said, "Keep going. You've got this."

I want to tell you about my struggles, the mistakes, the tons of lessons and all the mental toughness nuggets I've learned along the way to help YOU find the greatness inside of you and achieve more than you ever thought possible.

Mental Toughness Training Tip (right out of the gate)

Mistakes and setbacks are what taught me to succeed. I have learned my greatest lessons from defeat. Those lessons can be extremely tough and make you want to run the other way—but persevering through the challenges provides the lessons and strength to get to a higher level. Failures are actually necessary in order to grow and understand how to succeed.

AND SO IT BEGINS

"You throw like a girl!" Just five words I heard when I was five years old that have stayed with me ever since. I didn't really know exactly what those words meant—nor why my brothers would not let me play baseball with them and the neighbor boys. I *am* a girl, so why wouldn't I throw like a girl?

I ran to my mom crying. She told me that the boys were playing, but I could practice in the backyard with her. My mom was a strong woman, despite her petite size, and she didn't want me thinking that I would always have to stand on the sidelines. She instilled in me that someday I *could* beat the boys. She told me I could do *anything* if I set my mind to it. Go Mom!

She was bold during an era when girls were not allowed to participate much in sports at school because, after all, "girls could get hurt." Ugh! Instead, girls were supposed to stay inside to do household chores and learn to cook or sew. I knew that I would rather throw like a girl if it meant that I could have other options.

Thus, from a very young age, not only did my two older sports-enthused brothers exclude me in the neighborhood sports and games with their buddies, but they taught me that "boys do not like to be beat by girls—ever!" And more specifically, "Boys do not like to be beat *in sports* by girls—ever!" Period!

The passage of Title IX, a gender-based act, in 1972 prohibited discrimination based on sex in education programs and activities with more specific provisions added for sports in 1975.[1] It finally began opening doors for girls and young women to participate in sports in school. Title IX required schools to be proactive in ensuring campuses were free of sex discrimination in sports. Yes!

The whole process has been a slow go—but—there is no doubt that females have come a long way. We've improved dramatically as athletes and coaches with new opportunities to participate. In fact, today, it is actually considered rude for a boy to tell a girl that she "throws like a girl!" The old stereotypes have been mostly kicked to the curb, but an underlying current and certain presumptions remain. Those words may not be spoken, but some of the same feelings remain.

When girls win, it tends to be a blow to the male ego. Why? The old perceptions still exist that males are supposed to be stronger, bigger, faster, tougher, and more macho than women. Meanwhile, a female is typically thought of as *less* in all of these areas, making it impossible to measure up when it gets down to a physical- or sports-related activity. Additionally, and most importantly, females are still portrayed as *more emotional* than males—*not necessarily a positive attribute in this case.* Thus, males tend to believe they will dominate even more in pressure-filled situations.

> *Mental Toughness Training Tip:*
>
> *If you think you have less of an advantage because you are a girl, you will have less of an advantage because you are one. I never once thought that our women's teams had any less of an advantage. Plus, if you think you are not good enough, you will not be good enough. I never once thought that our team would not be good enough.*

WE CAME TO PLAY

I invite you on my journey that began in the late 1990's as the first and only female Head Women's Golf Coach in our Conference of universities and colleges (nine private institutions in Oregon and Washington).

I did not grasp the magnitude of the male-dominated hold in sports then, nor what it would take to win and build a successful championship program.

After working in the hospitality industry for ten years, I realized that dealing with the male ego went hand-in-hand with the old boys' club culture at the time. I never perceived a similar scenario would occur in the collegiate coaching world. I mean seriously—I was hired to coach *women*. My assumption was that coaching young women would *not* involve some of the same gender politics and stereotyping that I had seen in the business world. Boy, was I wrong! (Pun intended!)

I was initially hired as the part-time Assistant Golf Coach at a small private liberal arts college in Portland, Oregon. A female student at the school had shown interest in playing golf at the college and inquired why it only had a men's golf program. Interestingly, many colleges in our region had men's golf programs starting as early as the 1940's, but women's golf was completely off the radar. The emergence of the women's golf teams started almost 50 years later.

The passage of Title IX occurred in 1972, but it took time to be put into action. High school and colleges were required to comply by 1978[2] to fulfill a certain *equity ratio* with numbers of women and men in their sports programs. Athletic Departments were challenged to abide by the law or face serious consequences. The equity ratio improved, but it did take some time for schools to add more women's sports programs. This was the case at the college I initially went to work for which did not add Women's Golf until 1997.

With the new requirement to show equal opportunities for women in sports, schools had to figure out how to recruit more women to their athletic programs. The larger NCAA D-I and D-II colleges found the budgets to do just that and could hire full-time coaches to run their women's programs. However, the smaller colleges leaned on their football or basketball coaches to take on the women's and/or men's golf coaching job—or sometimes they hired a local golf pro to help.

I landed my first coaching job because my brother was the Athletic Director at the college at the time—he knew my passion for golf and the need for more women to serve in athletics. I interviewed with the Associate Athletic Director and was hired. Initially, I thought I was only going to be involved for a short time, but after a while, coaching young women golfers became my full-time passion. I loved it!

Eight years later, I was recruited to start a new D-III program about 25 miles away in Newberg, Oregon.

IT'S A PROCESS

No matter the division, maintaining a top collegiate golf program over several years is not like clicking the next episode on Netflix. The process involves an unshakeable amount of determination, hard work, and patience. These attributes must be combined with creativity and innovation to keep building and improving—especially a program without the benefits of athletic scholarships and where weather is not always your friend.

Obviously, if the road to success were easy, we'd all be at the pinnacle of our game. Many times, I wondered if the stress and anxiety from the many obstacles we faced trying to build and maintain a National Championship program was worth it—especially in a conference where no one believed it could be done.

The reality was my own fear and self-doubt kept popping in and telling me that maybe the other coaches were right—this may be impossible! I had to face my own inner resistance and encourage myself to keep going even when the road felt straight uphill. Passion is what kept me going.

Mental Toughness Training Tip:

Passion plays a huge role in achieving success. If you have a driving passion to accomplish something, you will work harder and you will achieve more! It's important to "get in the car!" Get onboard! There is a road to success—but it's not a straight one to the finish line. It will be winding, bumpy and uphill a lot of times, but it's there for you to drive.

THIS BOOK HIGHLIGHTS A STORY THAT NEEDS TO BE SHARED

I want to help athletes realize that it is *not* just mastering their physical skills that will bring greatness. *It is their mental strength and training that will determine excellence in their sport—and in life.* It is the belief in themselves down to their core that is key.

I want to inspire and reassure women who have an opportunity to coach youth and who might not feel qualified in a male-dominated field. You can do it! Men are not the only role models for children in sports. If you are a mother, stepmother, aunt, mentor for children, or other role, and you are not completely skilled at the sport, don't worry. What these young athletes really need is comradery, leadership, positive self-talk, role modeling and so much more you have to give.

And when you do win, it won't be easy either. Respect for women in sports (and in business) does not always come easy. Women need to remember to congratulate ourselves and each other for our successes along the journey. I have had to continuously remind myself that girls *can* win, *you* can win, and our team *can* win, when so many others did not believe in that possibility.

AN INSIDE JOB

Through many years of coaching and studying the mental side of golf, and sports in general, I have learned an incredible amount about what it takes to break through the resistance that can hold players back—the ego, self-esteem, emotional resilience, the subconscious mind, self-awareness, and confidence all come into play.

My experience has taught me over-and-over again that *mental toughness* is a necessary and critical component in achieving an elite level of performance—both as coach and player.

Mental toughness is no doubt a hot term used in sports these days. A few days before the 2023 US Open, a Golf Channel analyst, Jaime Diaz discussed the pre-US Open interview given by professional tour player Brooks Koepka and said: "Brooks thinks he's *mentally the toughest* on tour. He likes the chaos because he believes he will handle it better than anyone else."[3] Koepka has won five majors within six years, which is more than any other tour player.

But mental toughness is *not* something you achieve overnight. I have seen players repeatedly make the same mental mistakes. I have seen them battle their inner demons and blame their performance on the coach, a parent, the weather, another player, or something else that was bugging them. However, once they were able to overcome the incredible resistance that stood in their way and the big breakthrough finally happened, it was an inner discovery of confidence like no other!

Mental Toughness Training Tip:

Talent is not everything. Energy and mental toughness often surpass talent and experience!

When Girls Win, many times, the assumption from the male side is that something else must be in play—like maybe she's just a good recruiter or her budget is bigger. If the role is reversed, and a male coach wins, then *he* did a great job coaching his team. He has "great skills and an abundance of knowledge."

Over the years, as the team kept improving and winning, I had to dive even deeper internally. I worked harder on innovation and creativity as well as finding the mental skills to help myself and our team continue to grow stronger. My part-time job became unofficially full-time. It's just the nature of the work, and it takes time. Fortunately, I am completely passionate about my job.

Mental Toughness Training Tip:

Face the obstacles, observe your resistance, and you will be on your way to achieving success in whatever you undertake!

WANNA KNOW THE SECRET?

Just a few years ago, a new coach approached me on one of the more strategic holes at a conference championship event as we were both waiting for players to hit and asked rather confidently, "Are you a member of the LPGA?" When I responded no, he looked quite puzzled but didn't say anything further. I didn't pay much attention, as I was looking through my binoculars and preoccupied with my player who was hitting. When the coach got back in his golf cart to drive off, he hesitated and said over his shoulder, "Then you *must* be PGA?" I looked over at him, smiled, and replied again I was not. I knew at that moment that he was trying to figure out our secret in building a successful championship program. He kind of shook his head and sped off.

While I fully support both the LPGA and PGA and I have friends who are part of both, it hasn't been my affiliation with either that has helped me arrive where I am today. It's been a lot of reading and listening, mental toughness training, studying the game, observing what the best do better, innovation, and creativity. Those combined with many years of experience and learning from my own mistakes, setbacks, and challenges, asking questions, and using mentors, have helped me understand what it takes for *girls to win.*

One of the secrets? Everyone has the power within to succeed.

Please join me on this journey and discover just what it takes for girls to win. You will discover how joy will arrive in your heart even if you face a huge wall of indifference. With mental toughness training, instead of giving up, you will learn how to proceed full speed ahead to figure out a way to get through it. And that is when greatness truly finds you.

Special Nugget for When Girls Win!

When Girls Win, we learn how to bring out our best selves by under-standing the energy and vibe it takes to discover the great music that resides within. We believe the impossible is possible and our passion leads the way in helping us maneuver around the obstacles and break through the resistance.

WILL IT GO ROUND IN CIRCLES

I believe in the impossible because no one else does.

– Florence Griffith Joyner, World Record Holder, U.S. Track & Field

My competitive makeup and the challenges I faced in my youth helped me get where I am today. The lessons I learned early motivated me to challenge the status quo and always strive for more.

Call me "Miss Competitive." I can't lie; it's in my blood. People meet me and immediately pick up on my super competitive vibe. I never really thought I came across all that aggressive—I'm a high-energy, positive, and fun-loving person. Admittedly, my ambitious spirit runs deep and apparently, it really shows.

It might have to do with the fact that I have two older brothers who I was always trying to beat at various games. Or it might be because my dad was a professional boxer when he was young—he definitely instilled a drive in me. My mother also imparted strength in me and always encouraged me to reach for the stars.

All I know is that I have an incredible amount of fire when it comes to competing, and I make no excuses for it. It's just who I am: Someone who absolutely hates losing more than I love winning!

Actually, my rival spirit may also have been framed from my early years in grade school. I was a pretty smart kid, but one precocious boy in my class had a calculated way of edging past me in every class contest and project—every single time!

Instead of a backpack, this kid carried a small briefcase and wore business-attire as well as Poindexter-looking thick-rimmed glasses. Even in appearance, he seemed decades ahead of the rest of us. He would beat me at spelling bee contests, math showdowns, and he even took me down in art projects—which was my specialty! He showed up with his own gigantic set of colored pencils while I sported the basic box of eight crayons. Not fair!

When it came to science fair projects, I didn't stand a chance. Perhaps that's why he's a rocket scientist now and I am a golf coach. I am not complaining, as I am passionate about my coaching job—and I owe my former, now rocket scientist classmate for pushing me to be better and work even harder.

Every night after school, I would focus diligently on my homework because I was highly motivated to *not lose* the next day! I worried more about losing to this brainy classmate than focusing on a win.

Mental Toughness Training Tip:

*Motivation should always be stated in the POSITIVE! Abandon trying **not** to do something. The brain does not recognize the negative. You have probably heard the famous saying: "If you try not to think of a pink elephant, what comes to your mind?" Exactly: A pink elephant! I was always trying not to lose, and guess what happened? Yes, I lost. I should have been trying to WIN.*

I honesty did not realize just how competitive I was until I found myself at the eye doctor's office in fifth grade. I kept trying to read the bottom line of the vision chart while the assistant insisted that it wasn't necessary. She became quite annoyed with me when I continued to read the entire chart. I had this unshakable determination to beat the E Chart! Yikes! Clearly, my focus on winning had replaced my *trying not to lose* mindset.

I played a lot of different sports growing up, but golf became my passion. My dad was an avid golfer who helped me develop a love for the game. So many important lessons about life are learned on the golf course. One of my first lessons was that in order to play better golf, I had to lose my fiery John McEnroe-style temper that would emerge from nowhere when I missed a shot. Tennis great McEnroe's infamous reactions after a missed shot or a bad call were legendary. His famous line at Wimbledon in 1981 was when he yelled at the referee for a bad call, "You *can't* be serious!"[1] I hate to admit it, but that's pretty much how I reacted to my missed shots or losses on the golf course. Instead of yelling at the ref, though, I yelled those same words out loud to myself!

Mental Toughness Training Tip:

Remember that greatness is born from losing and failing. Every elite athlete suffers losses but learns from failure. Those lessons boost them to higher levels of achievement. Losing teaches resilience and makes you stronger for the next time—as long as you learn and grow from your setbacks.

THE BLAME GAME

And to think I used to blame my crazy emotions on being half-Italian. I figured that my genetic and emotional makeup were responsible for my wildly competitive nature. I have an Italian mother and although she did not have a temper per se, if I was in trouble—well, let's just say my dad was much easier on me than my mom. I know—it's not fair to blame my wonderful mother or the entire Italian population for my emotional outbursts on the golf course, but that's where I typically placed the blame.

Blame is something that arises a lot in sports. Our self-esteem takes a beating when we are not playing well, shooting well, performing well, or scoring well. Finding something or someone else to blame is common and much easier than looking inward. Our ego has a hard time accepting responsibility for a mistake or loss.

"Accettare la responsabilità, e non incolpare l'allenatore!" my mother would say to me. Translation: "Accept responsibility, and don't blame the coach!" NOTE: I especially love this line now!

Mental Toughness Training Tip:

Becoming more self-aware of your actions and reactions in competitive situations is super critical for growth and success! It always starts and ends with YOU. Accepting responsibility is crucial to taking your game to another level. Blame will not help.

SWEET EMOTION—NOT!

My first golf coach was rather surprisingly a nun, Sister Jêan Rose. She was also my college counselor at the all-girl Catholic high school, St. Mary's Academy in Portland, Oregon. Who knew that a nun could play golf? She was not the *Singing Nun* type, but more like Mother Superior from *The Sound of Music*—though she no longer wore a habit.

Sister J.R. shaped me up quickly. She told me that if I showed any more emotional outbursts during or after my rounds, she would not let me play—even if I was playing well and scoring well for the team! Wow, wake-up call! Thank you, Sister!

I had to find a way to calm down both on the links and when I finished playing—which I did. Unfortunately, this only created more internal knots of anxiety—not a good situation either. My stomach ached sometimes during tournaments and made me question whether golf was really all that fun anymore. If I didn't play well, I felt even more sick afterwards as I tried to stuff my emotions. I still enjoyed the team aspect of playing golf in high school and college, but my greatest challenge was how miserable I felt after making a mistake. I couldn't shake it off.

Slowly I found myself losing some of the enjoyment in the game that I loved so much. My coaches always told me that I had so much potential, and I worked extremely hard at the physical aspect of it. Unfortunately, the results on tournament day were sometimes just okay but most often fell short of my potential.

It wasn't until about ten years after college when I happened to have an opportunity to listen to a prominent sports psychologist, Dr. David Cook, the author of *Seven Days in Utopia*, and finally discovered the most important part of the game—in golf, sports and in life—*the mind!* He talked about how the mind is the "Great Separator."

When I was younger, someone gave me *The Inner Game of Tennis* by W. Timothy Gallwey—one of the very first books on the mental side of sports. But I didn't take it to heart—the content didn't seem to apply to me. My youth and my extreme naivete made me question why someone gave me a book on tennis when I played golf? Of course, now I get it. If I'd only studied that book when I was younger, I would have learned these lessons earlier.

I was under the impression that talent and outworking others was the absolute winning combination. I had no clue what an *inner game* meant or that we had two selves: Self One, the conscious and more controlling self; and Self Two, the subconscious and our innate abilities. Now, however, after many years of competing and coaching, I understand why some very talented and extremely hardworking athletes never reach their full potential or make it.

Around the time of this important mental discovery in the late 1990's, I started my first coaching role in women's golf. Even though I was beginning to understand that the power of the mind was the most important fundamental skill, understanding and doing were still two completely different things. Just like building physical skills takes time, the same holds true for shaping mental skills.

You can't just snap your fingers and become a mentally tough world-class athlete. It takes time to break old habits and create new ones that will invite your subconscious mind to work with you. There's so much more about the subconscious mind—the non-thinking brain that controls about 95 percent of what we do.[2] It plays a leading role in mental toughness—and unintimidated determination.

WHERE THE RUBBER MEETS THE ROAD

My first big mental—and emotional—test as a coach did not actually happen on the golf course. It was at my first coaches meeting at a conference fall tournament—where I was the only female coach.

The meeting was held at a basketball camp in a remote forested area in Central Oregon. There was one lodging facility for the teams and coaches in our conference—and conveniently located close to the host golf course. All the male coaches were staying together in a large suite, while the collegiate golfers were housed in two separate bunk houses —one for women and one for men.

But there was only the one suite for the male coaches, so as the only woman coach, I had to find an alternative place to stay. The situation was pretty awkward. I wanted to be near our team, but there was no place for me at the camp. After a lot of searching in this remote area, I finally found a small cabin about 15 miles away. This was not ideal, but better than a lone sleeping bag amongst the surrounding tall firs.

Most golf coaches in our conference at the time were coaching both the men's and women's teams. My college was one of the few that had a different coach for each golf team. All the colleges were trying to meet the Title IX requirement by offering golf for women, but it was simply not taken very seriously yet—especially at the D-III level.

Men's golf had been around for almost 50 years in our conference, first affiliated with National Association of Intercollegiate Athletics (NAIA) and then at the National Collegiate Athletic Association (NCAA) D-III level. At this time, the women's programs were just starting out. In fact, some of the first women's golf teams were created by finding interested students already enrolled at the college. Marketing a women's golf program to college prospects was simply not yet a priority at these smaller schools.

As the new kid on the block, I tried to be a silent observer among my male peers at this first meeting. But when I heard that the men's team players would be teeing off first both days ahead of the women, I felt the need to speak up. I strongly suggested they allow the women to go off first on the second day to equalize things both in terms of gender and weather conditions (i.e.: typically, less wind in the mornings in this area).

The negative comments that followed my suggestion almost knocked me out of my chair. It felt like I had dropped a match on gasoline and suddenly sparked a blazing fire in the room. Every coach was talking at once about how slow the women played, and how they would only hold up the men's teams. The male coaches quickly dismissed my idea. The next thing I knew we were taking a vote, and sure enough, the men golfers were going off first both days. My lone vote in this group meant nothing. Zero.

When the meeting was winding down and official business ended, many of the coaches continued their inner circle jokes as if I was not in the room. I am not sure whether it was meant to intimidate me, but I do know it came across as extremely rude. That's when I slammed my notebook closed with force as my emotions started to get the best of me. I wanted to let them know that I was beyond frustrated with what just occurred—and not going to tolerate it. No one seemed to notice.

I hustled out of my chair, gathered my things, said goodnight as politely as possible, and dashed out of what felt like enemy territory. I felt angry, frustrated, disrespected, dismissed, and outnumbered by the decisions being made without regard for our female players.

I also felt mentally drained after the three-hour meeting—like I had just finished a 72-hole tournament in one day. The clear message was that our women players were just along for the ride to take care of the Title IX requirement of the schools. The message? Women should feel lucky to even be allowed on the course.

As I stepped out into the darkness of the poorly lit camp, I spotted our school's 12-passenger van and rushed to jump in almost missing the long running board as I fell into the high-riding driver's seat. Even though I had only driven the large van two previous times, I felt compelled to crank the engine, step on the gas, and peel out of the parking lot in dramatic fashion.

Clearly, my darn emotions were taking over—sorry, Sister J.R.! I wanted to speed out of the parking lot and prove that I was a force to be reckoned with. Even though the men may have won this particular battle, they were not going to win the war. Game on!

Were my emotions helpful? No. What was my kickin' up gravel, speeding out of the parking lot antics going to prove to anyone? Of course, I knew this was not the most mature thing to do, but I did not have much mental toughness training at this point. I'd done it again—allowed emotions to rule the day.

What I have learned now (and wish I knew a long time ago) is that when emotion takes over in your body, it's much harder to think clearly. Cortisol—a hormone from the adrenal glands—rises, along with adrenaline, and can quickly cloud your thinking.

There is actual science behind what's happening when high emotion hits, as the cortisol hits your bloodstream and your heart rate and blood pressure rise at the same time. It's the natural fight or flight response that has kept humans alive for thousands of years when they were being chased by sabretooth tigers.

So here I am in my emotional fog—no sabretooth tiger in sight (thank goodness!)—and my not-so-brilliant plan takes a serious wrong turn. Literally. I proceed to take several laps around the camp, as I am desperately searching for my way out. Finally, one of the coaches strolls nonchalantly out of the coaches' cabin and points me toward the exit.

My hope of looking tough failed big time, and I felt completely humiliated. It doesn't get much worse! I don't know this for sure, but I suspect some of the other coaches were in the cabin peeking out the window and laughing hysterically as I sped around in circles.

In that moment, what I thought would deliver a strong signal of female toughness to my male peers was anything but that. It was like I proved to them my biggest fear I'd felt earlier in the meeting room: As a female, was I not good enough to be a coach?

Clearly, acting on negative emotions was not the answer—just like it's highly ineffective on the golf course or on your field of play. I survived but did not look good in the process.

Mental Toughness Training Tip:

Speeding around in circles is a good analogy for what can happen when emotions win the day. Emotional negativity has a physiological effect that clouds your thinking and decision-making ability. Plus, if your competitor sees you are upset, emotional, weak, and driven by ego, game over!

EMOTIONAL RESCUE

After tons of research to finally understand the physiological impact of raging emotions, I had a breakthrough. I realized that cortisol and adrenaline rush that occur in the body while emotions are flying can have a significantly negative physiological impact on performance.

I have worked hard with my players (and myself) on tactics to quickly let go after a mistake. Letting go of misses (mistakes) is imperative to thinking clearly and playing well.

"Neutral thinking means accepting that when something good or bad happens, it happens. Instead of getting caught up in the negativity, you accept it for what it is and move on," says author Trevor Moawad.[3] His point is that by releasing negative thoughts, your mind becomes free so you can perform better.

There are numerous mental tools to help control negative emotions. Mental imagery and mindset training, affirmations, visualization, mental rehearsal, meditation, and breathing are all powerful techniques. If you can visualize and breathe into your *good energy place* before a big performance and imagine playing from there the entire time, you will be better prepared for the challenges.

Imagery is like a rehearsal. The subconscious mind doesn't really know the difference between role playing and the real thing, so you can train it to handle tough situations that arise. The mind gets to know the drill and responds accordingly.

One imagery tool is to picture an invisible bubble around you to protect and shield you from unwanted vibes or negativity. Then, think of outside things that trap you emotionally. Is it fear of failure? Fear of not doing well enough? Fear of your parents being disappointed in you? Imagine those things coming at you and being deflected by your protective bubble. It sounds so simple, but it works. I use the imagery myself when it feels like negative arrows are zinging at me. My protective shield protects me, and it helps me to stay clear in pressure-filled situations.

Another critical tool when emotions are rising is to remember to breathe. The more you master deep belly breathing, the more you manage your cortisol level. You'll continue to make sound decisions and stay focused. This is not just two quick breaths–this is a minimum of five deep belly breaths to slow the heartrate.

The key is to practice visualizing how you will handle mistakes or emotional tests in advance of your competition, meeting, or whatever situation you're preparing for. This is an essential step that so many of us avoid. I see players honing their physical skills to prepare for competition, then foregoing the most important component—sharpening their mental game. Just like you train your body; you must practice your mental skills as well. That's the game changer.

Mental Toughness Training Tip:

Becoming mentally tough takes practice to create winning mental strength. Use imagery and visualization, journaling, meditating, breathing exercises, and affirmations to advance your game—on the course and in life. This sounds easy, but hard to do. Remember, practice is key.

Driving back all alone to our girls-only cabin that night in the big passenger van along a dark country highway lined with enormous and strong tall firs, is when I knew in my heart that I was there for a reason. I felt a deeper purpose and calling to support these young women student-athletes. I could sense they needed a female like me to stand up for them. I had to be a strong mentor, and have the courage to keep going, even in a male-dominated environment. At the same time, I realized that I also needed to learn how to be mentally and emotionally resilient in order to help the team achieve success!

Special Nugget for When Girls Win!

When Girls Win, we use our emotions to our *advantage*. It's important that we remember to breathe to lower our cortisol level so we can find our neutral place and return there when we feel negative vibes creeping in. Tipping your emotional hand gives away your power. Envisioning yourself staying calm and relaxed in the face of fear and failure is key to maintaining your power. Emotional resilience keeps cortisol levels down, so we can think clearly and fly higher than we ever thought possible.

3

TURN THE BEAT AROUND

I'm very proud to be a woman, but I don't want to be considered a great female athlete. I want to be a great athlete.

–Kerri Walsh Jennings, Three-time Olympic Gold Medalist, U.S. Beach Volleyball

I can't overemphasize the importance of emotional resilience to perform at your highest level—in anything.

I recently attended the US Junior Amateur at Bandon Dunes, where I witnessed a male player peppering us with the F-Bomb after hitting shots that he clearly was not happy about. All of us following the group could see that it was just a matter of time before more explosive streams of profanity would hit. Sure enough, another shot went awry, and he completely lost it. The kid had no chance. He was navigating a slippery slope of frustration and anger with his lack of perfection on the course, and when he couldn't take it any longer, it was all over.

Clearly, this young man could have benefited from a heaping dose of mental toughness training! That core fundamental is not for women only.

Being fiercely competitive is a good trait as it pushes you to constantly raise the bar, keep growing and prevents you from leaning on past achievements. At the same time, learning how to be *emotionally and mentally resilient* is critical to handling setbacks, mistakes and failures that inevitably happen. Reaching an elite level in your sport is not a straight road to the top, or more people would attain that, right?

Understanding that resilience is mainly how we handle the surprises, mistakes, errors, failures, distractions, interference, and unexpected frustrations along the way—it's an inner acceptance and the biggest part of the battle going on inside of us. Knowing these things will happen, accepting them and truly shaking it off is what elevates us to the next level.

> **Mental Toughness Training Tip:**
>
> *How you feel inside will reflect on the outside. When you react, you give away your power. When you stay emotionally resilient, you set up for success.*

I've always been taught the importance of controlling negative emotions—mostly thanks to my dad and my favorite nun! But let's face it: It's an ongoing process. We tend to resort back to what we know, and the habits ingrained in us. Clearly, I know I am not supposed to show negative emotions, so I've tried *not* to show negative emotions. But we all know that trying not to do something has the opposite effect. Why do our brains love the negative or the worst-case scenario?

GO WHERE YOU WANNA GO

Your subconscious mind does *not* differentiate between do and don't, because it doesn't recognize the negative. Remember the pink elephant? Psychologists refer to this as the "ironic process theory" in many mental training books, but most of us still tend to make this mistake. As humans, we are hardwired to inevitably think about what we want to avoid or what we don't want rather than what we want.[1]

The simple example on the golf course is to stand on a tee box, look around and see all the trouble spots where Heaven forbid, you don't want to hit it: penalty areas, out-of-bounds, bunkers, or any myriad of dangers. You think to yourself, "I don't want to go there!" But your brain does not hear the *don't*, so automatically starts thinking that *is* where you want to go. If you say to yourself, "Don't hit in the lake," it's an invitation to indeed "Hit it into the lake!" Dodging those negative thoughts is a challenge—the *ironic process theory* says if we try to suppress the thoughts, we'll just get more of them.[2]

So, what to do? You focus on what you *want* to do! Always return to your intention and what you *want* to focus on. In the case of the lake dominating the right side of the course, you could say instead, "That tree down the left side is the perfect target. I am going to hit my ball there" The fear of hitting the ball in the lake invites self-sabotage and causes you to inevitably hit it in the penalty area. Focus on what you *want* to happen!

Commitment is key to your success. Commit to what *you want* in order to avoid the *don't wants*.

When practicing, you can say what you want out loud, to make it even more powerful, effective, and committed. State your intention. Saying the words out loud will confirm the plan in your subconscious and help you with your process when you are competing.

> *Mental Toughness Training Tip:*
>
> *Focus on what you want. State things with intention rather than what you are trying to avoid. Always be committed to the outcome you want.*

KNOW THYSELF

In addition to commitment, *self-awareness* is a pivotal fundamental for performing at your highest level—and understanding your tendencies after you make a mistake.

If you lack the adequate self-awareness, you might not realize that your emotions are your biggest handicap. Some elite athletes may have success with the brooding, stay angry approach, but from my experience in working with athletes all these years, I know that anger and negative emotions will hurt you more than help you.

As you learn to understand your emotional triggers and become more self-aware, you can shift your thoughts to a higher vibration to pacify any anxiety, stress, tension, or fear that arises. Embracing a higher vibration is one of the most powerful things you can do to ensure winning energy and avoid a negative spiral.

Dr. Bob Rotella, a well-known sports psychologist who spoke at one of our National Golf Coaches' conventions, says self-awareness is a critical trait for achieving higher level mastery of your sport. If you aren't *aware* of how your emotions derail you at times, you will continue allowing them to rule the day.

HOW DO WE BECOME SELF-AWARE?

Esther Hicks, better known as Abraham Hicks, a celebrated motivational speaker and author—has developed an emotional guidance scale[3] to help you understand where your emotions are at any moment. This enables us to reach for a higher vibrational state. At the top of the scale are our highest emotions: gratitude, joy, and love, which bring higher frequency energy resulting in better performance levels.

THE EMOTIONAL GUIDANCE SCALE

1. Joy/Appreciation/Love/Freedom
2. Passion
3. Enthusiasm/Eagerness/Happiness
4. Positive Expectation/Belief
5. Optimism

6. Hopefulness
7. Contentment
8. Boredom
9. Pessimism
10. Frustration/Irritation/Impatience
11. Overwhelm
12. Disappointment
13. Doubt
14. Worry
15. Blame
16. Discouragement
17. Anger
18. Revenge
19. Hatred/Rage
20. Jealousy
21. Insecurity/Guilt/Unworthiness
22. Fear/Grief/Desperation/Despair/Powerlessness

The goal is to become aware of your emotional level—especially if your vibe is weak and then try to head up the scale. Everyone has different triggers that push them into a negative mindset and dim their vibe and path to success. Sometimes, you need to be proactive in getting to the top of the scale, especially if you're dwelling on mistakes and notice your vibration faltering.

Let's be honest: You are probably not going to jump straight from fear to joy at the snap of your fingers. But with self-awareness, you *can* figure out what works best for you under pressure. If you can escalate a little higher up the emotional scale, you will persevere and turn the beat around.

BREATHE. GROUND YOURSELF. REMEMBER YOUR LOVE OF THE GAME.

We had a player use this scale recently after a discouraging first three holes at a tournament. She found herself five over par after just three holes. Discouraged, she started thinking, "What emotion can help me get closer to joy right now?" She consciously decided to trust her ability and *believe* in her next shot. She went from #16 to #6 on the scale fairly quickly as she elevated her lower vibe. She began to *thrive in the moment*, have fun, and got right back in it with three birdies in a row.

She was mindful that she needed to tune to a higher vibration and regained her confidence to get back in the game. She finished strong in second place, just one stroke out of the medalist position.

On another note: avoid negative self-talk at all costs. "I'm just terrible today." "My game is no good." "I hate this putter." "I suck." All self-fulfilling prophesies. Be aware of that negativity creeping in and turn it around—STAT!

Mental Toughness Training Tip:

Radiating positive energy is one of the best ways to stay emotionally grounded. As your confidence escalates, you find yourself in the winners' circle more often. Growing stronger mentally takes time—consistently observing yourself and understanding what makes you tick and what triggers you are keys to competing and winning in any arena.

Special Nugget for When Girls Win!

When Girls Win, we continue to practice our emotional resilience when dealing with the small dramas in our lives, so we can be ready for the bigger stuff. It's easy to place blame on others, make excuses for our mistakes, and grouse about conditions. If we stay strong in our beliefs, focus on our intentions, and know that emotional resilience is our superpower in the most difficult situations, we have already won!

(4)

ROCK THE BOAT, BABY!

Never underestimate the power of dreams and the influence of the human spirit. The potential for greatness lives within each of us.

–Wilma Rudolph, Olympic Gold Medalist, U.S. Track & Field

Most coaches want to win. Most teams want to win. Some may have loftier coaching goals than others, but many are chasing the same dream as mine—to be the best we can be and win a National Championship. Sharing the same aspiration does not separate you from the rest of the pack, but the intention, energy and process you employ do. Set the bar higher, then get to work!

Mental Toughness Training Tip:

ALWAYS dream big! We all have callings but most of the time, we squash them down with excuses. If you are passionate and you want something, keep that energy, and go after it. Even if you fall short, you will have no regrets and will achieve much more than if you didn't try at all!

When I first started my coaching career, a top-ranked D-III team came to town from Texas to play in one of our local conference tournaments. This was the first time I had the opportunity to watch a female golf coach in action, other than when I competed.

Coach T and her team pulled up like a small cavalry with their top-of-the-line matching rain gear, umbrellas, and duffels, complete with personalized drawstring bags. They also had what looked like a giant food locker on the back of the coach's cart with snacks and water beautifully arranged. (Yes, I was snooping.). Our team, on the other hand, had no matching ensembles or umbrellas, or bags with logos and the only rain gear we had was from my personal closet.

Seeing this new highly competitive female coach, along with her organized and ambitious team ready to pounce on us, heightened my curiosity on how I could improve my own team. The coach was pleasant enough, but she made it evident from the moment we met that she was there to take care of business. I quickly realized that even though we shared similar competitive spirits, we were not going to be close friends just because we were both women. Nor, was she going to divulge her inspiring tips to help me become a top-ranked coach like her.

I wanted to learn from her and advance as a coach, but it was clearly not in her job description to teach me. Although Coach T did not become a personal mentor for me, I learned an enormous amount by just observing her in action with her team.

Unsurprisingly, the Texans delivered a wide margin crushing defeat against all of us in the Conference. No other team had a chance.

The day following the tournament, I had an important decision to make. I either had to accept that the Texas schools would always remain ahead of us with their undeniable warm weather advantage and appealing large budgets, or I could do something to change that narrative. I chose to get strategic to better position our team for dominance—though I had no clue how long that process might take.

Mental Toughness Training Tip:

Learn all you can from the best around you. Never think or assume you know it all—as that is ego-driven and will not improve your standing! Embrace a mastery mindset—learning and improving is important if you want to keep growing and advancing to another level. The rewards will eventually find you.

PULL IT TOGETHER

I had just witnessed how powerful a cohesive team look and presence were. So instead of moving the needle by adding more practices, I started with finding new gear! It's true. Looking good means feeling good and that is a competitive advantage on the golf course. I saw the pride in the Texas players with their full-on matching uniforms and school logo splashed all over them. Uniforms say, "I belong to a team, and we play together toward a common goal."

I met with our Associate Athletic Director and asked if we could buy uniform team rain jackets. I thought starting with a practical ask would be a good way to get to yes. After all, how could she say no to a core staple in the Pacific Northwest? She agreed to let me purchase new jackets but made it clear that I did not have a D-I budget. Where do you buy a small quantity of decent rain jackets with very little money to spend? I remembered one of our players had told me she saved a lot of money on her khaki golf pants by buying them at an army surplus store near campus, so off I went.

I was happily surprised to find that the surplus store not only had jackets in stock, but in one of our school colors—orange, and in this case, bright orange! Most importantly, they were at a super low price. Ironically, the exact number of jackets we needed was available. A sign? I immediately thought they were meant to be. One small problem, though, or *big* problem in this case—the jackets were only available in larger men's sizes. I laughed to myself, thinking if we aren't playing golf, we can inflate these jackets to float down the Willamette River! A multifunctional purchase indeed.

My first gear purchase as a coach posed a dilemma: Buy the jackets because they are the right price, even though they are oversized or take a chance trying to find the better sizes but at an exorbitant price. The easy answer: Buy the big jackets.

I was quickly learning in negotiations with our administrators that the low price always wins when you are a coach. Although not the most ideal first purchase, at least we would look like a team—and another bonus, we'll be easy to spot on the course!

Another lesson from Coach T: the importance of having morale-boosting snacks available for players. A five-hour competitive round without sustenance can be very draining—and college kids are not usually known for pre-planning their snacks.

As a new golf program, no one had thought about a budget for snacks and water during play. We had a stipend for dinner, but refreshments on the course were not included. In spite of that little hurdle, I decided to stop by a grocery store on my way to pick up the team and purchased a large bag of apples. I wanted to buy granola bars and Gatorade, too, but I knew I had to turn in the receipt, so apples were better than nothing.

When I unveiled the new jackets to the team, they were all laughs, although a few complaints about possibly looking like giant pumpkins. I still sensed their excitement in arriving as a cohesive squad. Simple matching jackets made them feel they were part of something more—playing for something bigger than themselves. They were pumped and just like that, school pride was a new part of our journey.

We arrived at the golf course with heads held high and a renewed sense of excitement. As they pulled their golf bags out of the van, I came around the corner with my bag of apples. From their reaction, you would have thought I had a bag of Halloween candy to accompany their pumpkin jackets!

As a new coach, I was particularly thrilled to have such elated players, feeling good and looking good—or relatively good in their matching jackets as they embarked on their competitive rounds.

Watching the team compete that day was completely energizing. I could feel renewed positivity in their mission and *our* mission. The players exuded confidence in how they walked and carried themselves —a sense of pride and team spirit reigned.

There's truly something to the *look-good, feel-good* theory as we shot our lowest round as a team that day. I was inspired by this newfound strength and self-confidence within our players. Who knew that over-sized rain jackets and a bag of apples could mean a higher performance level? I even found myself walking taller.

Mental Toughness Training Tip:

Success is in the details. Always pay attention to the details in everything you do. They can make a world of difference in elevating mood and a winning attitude. They can also be the difference in one or two strokes on the golf course (paying close attention to wind shifts on a golf course, low points of a putting green, etc.). Details rule.

YOU CAN'T PLEASE ALL THE PEOPLE, ALL THE TIME.

Unfortunately, my delight and enthusiasm quickly took a sharp, negative turn toward the end of the round, as I spotted the host coach speeding directly at me in his golf cart. Even from a distance, I could tell something was terribly wrong.

The players in my group had just finished teeing off on a short par 3 hole. As they were walking toward the green, the coach hit his breaks about 20 yards away from me, jumped out of his cart, and charged toward me. I was puzzled to see such displeasure on his face. I felt his angry vibe and aggression with each giant step he took toward me.

He stopped in front of my cart and in a hostile tone said, "Now look what you've done. We all have to buy rain gear and apples!" At first, I thought he's got to be kidding or that he was being sarcastic. Then, before I even had a chance to respond, he spun around, jumped back in his cart, and stormed off.

I had been riding along enjoying a bluebird-day as a brand-new golf coach, feeling like our team and I were making great strides together, when in an instant, a feeling of defeat washed over me. I started questioning myself and my purchases. Surplus store jackets and apples were a problem? Seriously? Whoa. And I thought I was late to the party.

I started driving toward the green feeling confused and unable to focus on my player who was now putting. In fact, I hit the brakes a little too hard, and they squealed as I drifted down the hillside. My player glanced over at me quizzically as I interrupted her putt. I knew my eyes were now watery and might reveal my sadness so I forced a smile, but I couldn't move from the cart. My mind went foggy as all I could think about was how angry that coach was toward me.

The people-pleaser in me felt dejected. I had tried to fool myself that it didn't matter if these coaches liked me or not, but now I had succumbed to wanting to keep the peace and make friends.

Taking this job was more stressful than I had anticipated. Initially, I thought I would be coaching with mostly women, swapping stories, and learning from each other, but clearly, that wasn't the case. My position as the only woman in this all-male community was altogether more challenging than I had expected.

After that jarring encounter, it became clear that I wasn't in this role to make new friends. In the end, we are all competitors. What was I thinking?

Mental Toughness Tip:

Let go of expectations! You can expect to perform well but know that situations arise that you cannot control. You can never control how anyone else acts or performs. Shine your own light. Focus on YOUR greatness. And above all, keep the big picture in mind.

IT'S A HOME GAME.

I knew at this early point in my coaching career that I had to rise up, stay focused, motivate the team, and help them grow—all while feeling good about myself even if I wasn't well-liked by my peers. I learned to maintain my strong positive energy despite the negativity or intimidation tactics of some of my male peers. If I felt bad about myself or not good enough, that was on me—not them. I had to remember it's a home game.

I also learned that trying to earn respect from my coaching peers was not a necessary—or winning—goal. As much as I wanted to earn respect from the guys, deep down, I knew that respect had to come from within. It would not come from the validation of others around me.

My early revelation that men do not like to be beat by women, especially in sports, kept me wondering whether I had a chance at building a successful National contending team. But...as my mom had taught me as a young girl, you never have to accept standing on the sidelines. Step into the arena and show 'em what you got—regardless of gender!

I needed to make choices that aligned with my goal—to build the team, improve our skills and mental toughness—compete well and win. I knew I needed to stand tall in the arena and go for it full throttle or settle for average. I chose to stand tall and became a force to be reckoned with!

My mom always said that most of the greatest work was achieved by those who were told that they didn't stand a chance but found the determination and still believed they could. And as Serena Williams once said, "You have to believe in yourself when no one else does."[1]

I personified *change* for the other coaches. Just as I was struggling to fit in to the boys' club, their discomfort with me—and change—was visible.

Marketing guru and author, Seth Godin, will be the first to say that change is an opportunity. He says change creates tension, which can make some people feel uncomfortable and even cause panic.[2] That's why many people resist change and prefer to remain in the status quo. For some, remaining in autopilot is easier than shaking it up with innovative ideas to improve the organization.

But guess what? Zero advancement comes from remaining on autopilot. Own your talent, let your light shine, and step out of your comfort zone. That is the only option if you want to reach a higher level.

Mental Toughness Training Tip:

You cannot control what others think of you. Stay on your path with a positive mission in mind. When someone vents something intentionally hurtful, shake it off and remember that YOU are meant to be there to do powerful, transformative work. Show up, endeavor to grow, and voice your ideas. You possess greatness and were born to shine.

Special Nugget for When Girls Win!

When Girls Win, we are unapologetic about who we are and unafraid to stand tall, rock the boat when we need to, and radiate. Women have been in supporting roles for a very long time and finally understand that it's okay to be bold, to pursue our passion, and be a competitor in the arena. It's okay to embody strength, passion, and finish as a winner. Be courageous and success is yours!

DON'T STOP ME NOW

People would say, 'Girls don't play hockey. Girls don't skate.'
I would say, 'Watch this.'

–Hayley Wickenheiser, Gold Medal winner, Canada women's hockey

"Are you going to be doing your coaching thing again today?" I heard those words often from my male peers in my early days as a coach. That was more than 20 years ago when I found myself in a unique situation as the only female coach.

Many of the coaches had a routine of playing a round of golf in front of the men's and women's collegiate golfers at tournaments. They'd finish their rounds and then be there for their players when they were coming in on the 18th hole. I didn't understand this routine, as I was with my players in the practice area—yes, doing my coaching thing— and had no clue that some of the other coaches were teeing off first.

I assumed the other coaches were spread out on the course, watching their players compete. Just two tournaments in, while I was coaching my player on the 4th hole, a competitor in the foursome I was with, started waving at a group of male golfers teeing off across the fairway. She turned and announced to the group, "That's my coach!" *Wait, what?* I thought to myself. No one said anything to me about enjoying a round as a coach. I was really confused and thought it was so odd. I wondered why those coaches were not out with their players?

The tournament was held at a beautiful country club and the thought of playing the course was certainly appealing. But I didn't understand their rationale. I knew that my job and passion were with our players. That's what I was hired to do. So, I shrugged my shoulders watching my peers tee it up and moved on with the team.

Golf coaches made very little money in those days compared to other sports—not that we make much these days! And most golf coaches—myself included—had other jobs, so I suppose the opportunity to play free golf at some nice courses was an extra bonus. When I accepted this first coaching job, nobody mentioned the perk of playing golf during tournaments. Perhaps the other coaches had different agreements with their athletic departments?

At first, I felt like I was doing something wrong in wanting to be out on the course watching my players rather than teeing it up with my new male counterparts. I had a debate constantly spinning in my head at tournaments on what was the right thing to do.

As the new kid—and only woman—I felt a deep need to fit in and be accepted by my peers. At the same time, this idea about possibly playing sounded pretty interesting; to be able to both coach and work on my own game could make for a pretty fun job.

PLAYING WITH THE BOYS

What if the guys ask me to join them? I didn't even know if they would, but I wanted to be mentally prepared just in case. The thought of teeing it up with my male peers was intriguing, and I also knew as a woman, that teeing it up with a group of guys could present additional challenges other than taking me away from supporting my players.

Playing golf with my dad over the years taught me a lot about playing in an all-guys foursome. Often when we'd go out to play without a tee time, we would get paired with another twosome—and 99 percent of the time that meant two other men. I didn't usually care who joined us, but the additional guys usually thought otherwise. Several times I overheard them say, "Oh no, we have to play with a girl!"

Golf was definitely dominated by men while I was growing up. Many women were just getting into the game, so it was typically assumed they were not very good and slower players because they were beginners. The immediate assumption was that I would hold up the group.

It felt very similar to my early days when my brothers and the neighbor boys did not want me to play baseball with them. The baseball boys didn't think I was good enough to play with them. The golfing boys pretty much thought the same thing, but the difference was in this sport, they didn't have a choice in the matter as the pro shop had paired us together.

When we joined a group and I hit it okay, but did not score well, the round would typically go just fine. However, if I was doing better than the men in our foursome—other than my dad who was always cheering for me—or if I hit from the men's tees and drove it past one of the guys, the round did *not* go well. Men seemed to fear either losing to a girl or exposing their own weaknesses in front of me. I don't know this for certain, but I concluded that many men preferred not having the extra social pressure of playing with a female—especially one they did not know.

Here's the other thing: they may have felt uncomfortable, but how do you think I felt? Knowing that you are going out to play a sport you love with people who would rather not be in the same group with you is not fun.

Mental Toughness Training Tip:

You will face uncomfortable situations in sports, business, or at various times in your life no matter what. Understanding and learning how to accept them and staying within your own zone will only make you stronger and likely lead to the best outcome.

BUCK PEER PRESSURE

For the next few tournaments, I was so preoccupied about the possibility of joining my male peers that I went ahead and tossed my clubs into the van just in case I was asked to play. I also thought if I *was* invited, I could compromise and play just 9 holes. Meeting my peers halfway seemed like a good idea to solve my need to belong while still coaching my players for part of their rounds.

At long last, the much-anticipated scenario arrived—the coaches popped the question. As much as I wanted to say yes, I just couldn't do it. Sure, I wanted to be accepted—don't we all? But I would be in direct conflict with our team's goals and quite frankly, the reason I was there in the first place. I kept thinking: How can I get our team to a stronger and higher level if I am not fully committed to supporting them while they are competing? Going half the distance was not responsible to the players, nor to our mission as a team.

At each tournament, I was finding the time I spent with my players extremely useful—powerful connections were being made, we were learning course strategies, new creative shots, and using the USGA rules to our advantage. We were playing trouble shots well, and I was understanding more and more the mental resilience necessary to elevate our team to the next level.

These young women were taking their games seriously and wanted to be competitive at collegiate golf. It was important to them, and it was important to me. We needed to stick to our goals and strategies as a team to continue to progress.

As a new coach—and experienced player who had been coached—I knew that observing the team and being present for them was important to our master plan to improve and grow. I also wanted to experience what my players were feeling so I could better understand how to help them, mentor them on shots and overall course management, as well as mindset and mental strengthening processes.

I didn't quite understand the powerful message initially, but later realized that I showed my players we were all in it together when I was out there with them and in the end, it made them all want to practice and fight that much harder to keep improving.

This scenario is similar to Peloton instructors who tell you they are your *workout partners* while pedaling and sweating through the workout with you. "We can do this! I am in it with you! Just 20 minutes to go!" A unique appreciation and bond are formed between the participant and instructor.

It's your action—not just the words—that builds a Championship program.

Lesson learned.

Coaching goals at the D-III level have changed since then. Just meeting Title IX requirements doesn't cut it anymore—thankfully! Today, the pressure is on to build successful award-winning programs. We've broken the mission impossible barrier and continue to excel and achieve more.

Mental Toughness Training Tip:

Believe in your goals and own your own game. It might feel cool to be accepted by your peers, but is that worth sacrificing your ultimate pursuit? Putting in only half the work, energy, effort, and commitment will not advance you to your goal. Your personal journey and the why of what you're doing are key to your success. Why do you get up in the morning? Why do you pursue your sport? In the end, your persistence—

and honoring your passion—are what will help you fly higher and farther.

RISE ABOVE

Funny thing, but my choosing not to play in the boys' club became a running joke for a few of my peers. I continued to be invited to play at several tournaments and each time I declined, I would hear the line all over again: "Are you going to be doing your coaching thing again today?"

At first, I have to admit, their sarcasm stung. I didn't know if this was a psychological tactic to make me feel more excluded, a stereotypical taunt to imply I'd never achieve my goals, or a subconscious ploy to annoy me and raise self-sabotaging emotions.

I was still learning my own inner game and how to be mentally tough, so I struggled at times with some ongoing self-doubt, but I decided my only choice was to accept the reality and move on. Once I accepted *what is*, I was able to let go and walk away with renewed energy. I said to myself confidently: "Yes! I will stay focused on the team today."

I intentionally walked a little taller and used my body language to feel good and position myself. In those moments, I could feel both my goals and our team goals getting much closer. I was discovering how to convert my uncomfortable emotions—and this awkward ongoing gender dilemma—into a much greater advantage than I even realized at the time.

> *Mental Toughness Training Tip:*
>
> *Running from negative emotions will only give them more strength and divert you from your mission. The key is to know why your passion drives you, so negative emotions will not sway you from your goal. You hone your inner game and commitment to rise above the fear of not being good enough or fitting in.*

Every time, at every tournament, when I said, "no, but thanks," I began channeling my emotions differently, which helped me gain an incredible amount of mental strength. And the big bonus? By physically being out there on the course with my players, it gave them more encouragement and strength. They knew that I was in it to win it with them—like the Peloton instructor—and that helped them develop more confidence. When I followed my gut instincts on best practices as a coach, I experienced powerful fuel to amplify our team's focus on what we needed to accomplish to win.

I believed in my work as a coach even more, and discovered a mental toughness I didn't even know existed. I was letting go of my need for approval, to fit in and to be liked, especially as the only woman—and I knew I was doing the right thing for me and our team.

Accepting the reality of the situation, and then committing, believing, focusing, and sticking to the ultimate goal allowed me to release my need to be liked. The experience also taught me the extraordinary inner strength available if you believe and trust more deeply in yourself *and* your purpose. Once I figured out that I didn't need to be anything more for my peers, I was able to shift into a higher gear and never look back.

Acceptance—acknowledging what is—is a powerful tool. Remembering what you *can* control, and what you *cannot* control is a dynamic force. Just like I accepted that the guys were going to query me on my coaching, you also must accept the conditions of your game on any given day—whether it's who you're paired with, the weather forecast, or any myriad challenges.

Sure, self-criticism and ego muscle into your awareness trying to sabotage your mindset and make us question ourselves. Let it go. Face the reality and rise above.

Mental Toughness Training Tip:

Understand—and release—what you can't control. Period. So many things are out of your control: the weather, what others think of you, your pairings and playing partners, the wind, course conditions, and pin placements. You name it. Focus on what you <u>can</u> control—your attitude, your mindset, and especially your belief in yourself!

WHEN ADVERSARIES BECOME YOUR BEST TEACHERS

What those male coaches did not realize during this critical time in my early coaching career is that *they* had actually become my best teachers. They weren't bad guys; they were just on a different path than mine. I learned how to be stronger and stay in my own lane while finding my zone. Thank you adversaries for the lessons.

My favorite quote by Ralph Waldo Emerson comes to mind: "Do not go where the path may lead, go instead where there is no path and leave a trail." I was learning from these peers and this experience to forge my own way and leave a trail.

Mental Toughness Training Tip:

Always remember that your adversaries are your best teachers. Big lesson here. You can get angry, upset, frustrated, whatever, but they can teach you more than you ever imagined. Pay attention to what your rivals are teaching you. There's no mistake they are on your path for a reason. Be aware. Learn the lessons—and use them to your advantage. Trust me, you'll grow immensely and emerge victorious.

BE CURIOUS, NOT JUDGMENTAL

As our team improved and stayed true to the game, the pressure on the other teams to grow ramped up big time. We had raised the bar.

Eventually, the coaches' golf games at tournaments came to an end. Other coaches saw the benefit of coaching from the course in order to advance their players as well. That didn't mean that all the coaches were necessarily happy about this new change—I overheard grumbling for quite some time. I didn't want to be the bad guy—or the bad gal in my case—but the overall transition was a positive step for all of our players.

As most coaches acknowledged that focusing on their players was the right thing to do, my reputation as an outsider remained. Not long after this coaching transformation, a coach came up to me at a tournament and actually asked me if I was ever going to leave my job to have kids. He seemed sincere, but I was surprised at the personal nature of the question. It caught me off guard. "I highly doubt it," I mumbled and abruptly walked away. I learned later that some coaches thought I was a short timer and that I would leave to have children—but they knew nothing about me.

One of my favorite scenes in the popular show, *Ted Lasso,* is when Coach Ted makes a wager in a bar playing darts with the villain, Rupert, the former owner of the AFC Richmond team. Ted acts like he's not great at darts, throwing with his right hand at first and missing badly. But when it comes time for the match, he says, "Oh that's right —I am left-handed," as he switches hands and easily scores a bullseye, winning the bet. "If you knew me—you would have known that yes, I play darts," he quips, quoting Walt Whitman, "Be curious, not judgmental."

Sometimes we assume we know the people we are working with and make incredibly misguided judgments about them. The other coaches did not realize my medical history or my strong passion for coaching and mentoring young women.

Mental Toughness Training Tip:

Shrugging off what others think of you is so important to personal growth and building confidence. No one knows what you may be going through. Always focus on your own goals and never let peer pressure and judgment impact your journey.

And most of all, remember the key fundamentals for achieving your goals:

1. *Accept yourself*
2. *Look inward not outside for approval*
3. *Do the work*
4. *Be persistent*
5. *Know your WHY*

Special Nugget for When Girls Win!

When Girls Win, we are focused on our own goals and worry-free about what others think. We release our people-pleasing insecurities and needs, so we can pursue and achieve our dreams, goals, and wins. With a deep-seeded belief in ourselves and our mission, we know that our dreams are possible and in time, we arrive to shine our inner greatness.

We also understand that we can channel negative emotions, like anger or frustration, into intense positive fuel to help us accomplish our mission. We achieve a higher level of success as we become true to our authentic and true selves—and less to ego. We own our game, our journey, our power, and ultimately, the greatness that we all have within us. This is not about arrogance—but using our gifts and talents to continue to climb to new heights.

6

GOOD, GOOD, GOOD VIBRATIONS

True champions aren't always the ones that win,
but those with the most guts.

–Mia Hamm, Olympic Gold Medal, US Women's Soccer

E arly on in my career, we had a new player arrive who had nothing but grit, determination, and a take-no-prisoners approach to her game. She quickly earned the nickname *Bulldog.* She came to practices fired up with a competitive air and was ready to win all the contests I teed up for the team. Whenever we had our stars contest for chip-ins, closest-to-the-pin, up-and-downs from bunkers, she was determined to rake in all the stars.

But something happened at one conference championship. I noticed her entire mood, mannerisms and body language were drastically different—kind of deplete and energy-less. She seemed zombie-like and lacked her typical go for broke attitude.

She finished the first round of 18 with a decent score but just hadn't attacked the course as usual. When I asked about her lack of enthusiasm, she told me she just wasn't feeling it that day like she did at practice. In fact, she said she felt bored with her game, like she was just going through the motions.

START ME UP

After our discussion, I realized she had fallen well below her usual gutsy energy level that day. Everyone has an optimum intensity level where they play their best—a combination of tension and excitement. Some athletes need to fire themselves up a little more and others might be too pumped up or anxious and need to calm themselves down (i.e.: me!).

It's been determined by research that on a scale from 1 to 10 (1 being relaxed and 10 being tense), the best place to be for golfers is somewhere between 4 and 6.[1] For football players, it might be 6 to 9 for best performance. That day, my player was most likely under 3.

If that ideal amount of fire is not present or too low, or conversely, if the flame is too high, peak performance will be harder to achieve. The important key is to find what works for each player, and develop methods to stay at that cadence. It's particularly important before the round (tournament, game, etc.) to get to that optimal energy place.

At first, the player wasn't sure if she could get there but we agreed on some visualization techniques, and she listened to her favorite pump-me-up music before the final round. It may sound so simple, but it worked. She visualized the final round being more like a practice and envisioned herself driven, focused, and owning each shot. She brought an extraordinary conviction and intention that day and actually came from several strokes behind to shock the field with a win at the championship!

Now, visualizing, listening to pump-up music, and believing you're truly in your zone does not necessarily guarantee a victory. The lesson is that knowing where your energy level needs to be, and understanding what motivates you will help you play at highest efficiency level to achieve your best potential each time you play.

This player performed at her best when she was a little more fired up. When she started feeling lackadaisical and spiritless, she did not perform at her highest level which led to carelessness and unnecessary mistakes. It's not a swing breakdown, rather an intensity breakdown.

I didn't know if our Bulldog could win that day, but I knew if she could remain exhilarated and in her high-energy place, she would be in striking distance. As she became aware of her need to be more excited to perform (like her practice sessions), she found her ultimate stride, and performed to her potential to score her first victory!

Of course, in a sport like golf, where a competitive round can take up to five hours and you need to rest your mind while walking between shots, Bulldog couldn't stay at full throttle the entire round. She had to learn to rest her mind, but then be right back into it. Her process trained her to pump herself up before she hit.

Mental Toughness Training Tip:

From 1 to 10 (1 being relaxed and 10 being tense) what is your ideal energy level when you are performing at your best? Once you know your ideal performance number, you can adjust with tactics for when you're feeling too low or too intense. To inspire yourself, have a motivational phrase or song in mind even if you have to sing the anthem to yourself! If you're amped or anxious, deep focused breathing is the best technique to slow your roll. Getting to your optimum rhythm enables you to compete at higher levels more consistently.

GOT ME UNDER PRESSURE

The next year at our Conference Championship, another top player was struggling on her last few holes of the final round. She knew she had a chance to win the Championship and the pressure was intensifying as she was getting closer to the final hole. This player was succumbing to doubt that she could really get it done.

The negative forces were interfering with the intense and determined energy she had exuded all day. I observed her from across the fairway and could immediately tell that she was feeling down as I watched her shoulders slump while she was walking off the 17th green. I did not know specifically where she stood in the tournament, but her lowered head and hesitant posture clearly expressed defeat.

We did not have live scoring then like we have now, but I knew the scores had to be close, and I was fairly certain that my player still had a chance to win. But I had no idea how many strokes stood between her and the competition for the number one honor.

I had to figure out a way to get this athlete back on track. At first, I said nothing and just walked silently with her as we approached the 18th hole. The Championship was hosted at a resort course in Central Oregon that typically required golf carts, so the distance between greens and tee boxes was much longer than normal. The longer walk worked to my advantage when suddenly a song I had heard on the radio that morning popped into my head. Figuring I had nothing to lose, I turned to her and started singing the chorus, "I get knocked down, but I get up again. You are never gonna keep me down, I get knocked down, but I get up again, you are never gonna keep me down."

I know—probably not the best song a top sports psychologist would recommend in a high-intensity performance moment, but I had to try something to snap my player back to her happy place a la *Happy Gilmore*! She needed an energy boost and those words seemed to fit. The minute she heard the song, she started laughing—at me and with me—and I could see her shoulders relax and her stride become more determined.

She turned and looked at me and quietly asked, "What do you think?"

"Trust will get it done," I replied.

PICKIN' UP GOOD VIBRATIONS

We had just one hole to go and she was rallying her good vibes back. She crushed her drive down the middle, hit a great second shot and an approach shot to 10 feet. She then finished the 18th hole sinking the 10-foot putt for birdie. She won the Championship by one slim stroke— and then went on to become the National Freshman Player of the Year, the first ever national award for a woman in our Conference. She brought the confidence, trust, and intensity on that last hole to win it all.

Now, you might be wondering was it is my singing that has been our team's secret sauce after all these years? I wish that was the case as I love music but should never (ever) be allowed to sing in public!

No, singing is not the secret, but being aware of your tendencies and how to optimize positive energy are probably the most important factors for any athlete. I knew that my player had lost her positive spark right along with her confidence. Her highest and best vibe had dropped below her optimal zone, and she had to reboot.

One of the best ways to refresh your mindset is to enlist a powerful motivational mantra, like *You got this, girl! You can do it! You're strong in the face of adversity.* And of course, you can always sing a tune that pumps you up. *Hall of Fame, Unstoppable, Turn the Beat Around* and *Eye of the Tiger* work quite well!

And if you're feeling over-amped, it's important to compose yourself with deep, slow breathing. Deep breaths slow the heart rate and tame the nerves so you can stay centered and grounded.

Mental Toughness Training Tip:

Be sure to have a personal mantra or inspirational tune to help you ramp up your winning energy. If you're in over-drive, remember deep breathing will slow your heart rate and ease you back to your zone. Breath is a dynamic power source. If you are feeling anxious, with just a few deep breaths, you can help to maintain the best cortisol level for performance. The 4-7-8 breathing method[2] seems to be one of the best methods used for athletes. Inhale to the count of 4, hold for 7 seconds and then exhale for 8. Give it a go—it works!

FREE TO BE ME

Every athlete is different. A coach's ultimate job is to understand what motivates and prepares each player so they can perform at their highest level. Indeed, a big challenge sometimes. In fact, I used to mistakenly assume that most players are like me and a little too fired up. I thought spa-type music would be perfect all the time before big events. But I came to understand that different players needed to ignite the fire while others needed to douse it a bit before they teed it up.

I played relaxation music in the van and read a short relaxation script from top sports psychologist, Dr. Morris Pickens, before we won our first NCAA trophy in 2013. While that strategy worked well for the 2012-13 team as we finished taking home our first hardware for fourth place, it did not resonate at all with the next season's team. Rather, it mellowed out some of our new players who were quite ready to take a nap by the time we got to the course.

They knew I was so excited about our team's spa tunes but eventually confessed that this calming vibe was simply not working and was squashing their energy and enthusiasm way too much. At first, I was bummed that my go-to meditative playlist just wasn't it for this new team. It definitely would have been easier to stick with that routine, but as a coach, you have to figure out what is the best for your current players in any given moment and you must adjust. Just because it worked before, does not mean it works again.

Note: If you have a personal ritual or routine that works for you it's invaluable to keep in your arsenal.

Mental Toughness Training Tip:

Self-awareness of your optimal energy level is critical to performing at your best. Understanding your own needs, what inspires you and how to return to your best optimal energy state are key to improving and winning. We are all motivated differently, learn differently, and have different levels of excitement and energy. There is no one-size-fits-all solution.

Special Nugget for When Girls Win!

When Girls Win, we know that self-awareness is key to our success. We know how to get to our personal zone to perform at our highest level. We also know that maintaining our best personal energy level is key to our success.

GONNA FLY NOW

They say discipline and dedication and respect are the key factors,
but patience is a virtue that is absolutely essential!

–Ria Ramnarine, Professional Boxer

Trinidad and Tobago's first female World Champion

When I was first hired to start and coach the new women's golf program at a Christian university in Newberg, Oregon, I brought all my high energy and was ready to blast off as quickly as possible. I had developed a great deal of confidence from all my earlier coaching experience, and I knew I had great support behind me from the university's administration. I was completely ready and prepared to show the world that women's golf was just as exciting as football!

I was in an unusual hurry to make it all happen. In my world, building a successful program couldn't happen fast enough. My fast timeline was born of an incessant need to prove myself as a coach and also as a woman in the sports arena.

As I've mentioned, not only was I the first female coach in our Northwest Conference, but I was just the *second* female coach at this university (first female coach since the school joined the NCAA in 1998). What's very unusual is the university chose me to start the women's golf program before the men's golf program even existed. I felt honored but also intense pressure to succeed—STAT! No one was pressuring me but myself. The pressure was totally on me. There was no option but to just do it.

The university originally wanted me to wait a year to launch the program when I was hired in the spring of 2006, but I wanted to jumpstart it that fall. I should note that collegiate golf is a two-season sport, playing in the fall and spring. I was eager to get going and after finding a couple of solid recruits for the fall 2006 season, I begged the Athletic Director to let us hit the links sooner.

It takes four players to create a team score, and normally a team consists of five players. The best four out of five scores are used for a team score. I was willing to settle for four players to launch the program and post our first score as a team. I put up recruiting signs around campus hoping a few young women might own some clubs and want to play. Surprisingly, two members of our nationally ranked women's basketball team came knocking on my door.

They had been a Godsend to our school and now to our inaugural golf program. These competitors, one a junior and the other a senior, became the backbone in developing and building our championship program as well as defining our influential team culture right out of the gate. Their abilities on the golf course didn't quite match their outstanding moves on the court, but their work ethic, maturity, commitment, driving passion and advanced leadership skills helped establish the platform from which our team would grow.

ONE LOVE, ONE HEART

As I thought about what it takes to build an exemplary team, a quote from marketing guru Seth Godin came to mind. *"Culture is at the heart of whether you are going to get to where you want to go or not."*[1]

There is no doubt that a strong culture is the foundation of any sports program. Many coaches will say that process is what drives results, but I have learned that culture is the key driver. It is extremely important to establish your values and mission from the beginning as the core of the team and its culture.

It's the character and chemistry of the team that make the difference.

At that point in my career, I did not understand yet how important chemistry was. But I can tell you for certain now that chemistry is absolutely essential to compete at the National Championship level and to build and maintain an elite program.

Many believe that in a sport like golf, it just takes a few talented individual players who can score, and that chemistry is not as influential. Sure, each player is on their own to score, but if the players are only out for themselves and not competing as a team, you'll never achieve a thriving cohesive and passionate team culture. It's the connectedness that wins championships.

The building blocks of our new program started with positivity, high-energy, learning resilience and an ongoing focus on what we were doing well. I learned that adding up 3-putts or greens missed or talking about what went wrong immediately following a tournament could be too detrimental. Replacing *what went wrong* with *what did you learn* was much more valuable and became a big part of our improvement plan. Also, understanding our university's mission of excellence and focusing on our values as a team were key to our successful program. That focus and commitment were the cornerstones of our achievements and reaching a higher level of play every year.

Each new player learned quickly that they were following in the foot-steps of earlier teams who built a powerful legacy of hard work, consistency, attitude, grit, and a ton of patience. My job as coach is to continue to instill those attributes. I resisted my personal need to sprint and hustle the results along and committed to allowing it to come together rather than trying to force it to happen!

Mental Toughness Training Tip:

It's critical to stay patient with the process and know that building the blocks of consistency wins. It's not a sprint but a continual marathon to growth and improvement.

BRING IN THE BALLERS

I learned a great deal from the first two talented basketball players on our inaugural team. Their personal commitment and dedication to hard work and excellence laid the groundwork for our success. When I asked if we should cancel practice due to foul weather, they said that canceling was not an option—which meant I had to get creative and figure out a way to keep building and improving our team every day, even if we didn't have an indoor facility at the time.

As expected, rain arrived, and I scheduled a conference room for our practice that week. I brought in a small putting green to practice on. We just had the four players on our initial team, so it seemed like an easy way to get a little work in. After they each made 10 putts in a row, they wanted to know what was next. I wasn't sure. The ballers suggested, "We could go to the gym and run lines." The faces on our other two players immediately registered a hearty *no thanks*. Instead, I held my first mental toughness session—and little did I know then the impact this meeting would have on our program.

I can't help but add what it was like handing out the uniforms to our star basketball players, now turned legitimate golfers. They couldn't stop laughing when they opened up their duffel. Their sentiment? "Do we really play a sport wearing a skirt?" Yep, new khaki skorts and navy polos. Our first uniform.

In the end, these basketball players helped me innovate our path to greatness. They were ballers who knew the amount of hard work it would take to build a championship program. Even though they—and their tenacious teammates—knew they most likely would not be on the first team to go to Nationals, they were all committed to leading the way for others to be a part of that journey in the future. Our first team—the Fab Four—was comprised of selfless warriors who understood what the bigger picture and purpose was all about. That's what it takes. A committed group of pioneering spirits who are in it to build a lasting team and enduring culture.

BUILD ME UP, BUTTERCUP

During these initial few years, we also worked hard to market ourselves as a program. We found some amazing supporters who helped better fund our program so we could travel outside of our conference and hold a tournament in the sunnier climate of Phoenix, Arizona.

One of those supporters is former PGA tour pro, Brian Henninger, and the Henninger Foundation, who donated $8,000 to allow us to accelerate. Another is former CEO of Portland General Electric and alum, Peggy Fowler (and her husband Bob), who supported us from the beginning and eventually helped us with a new indoor center. Those connections played an important role in helping us build and learn more quickly what it was going to take to reach our ultimate goal— earn a berth at the National Championship.

In just three years, we became Co-Champions in our Conference. Then, with a high ranking in our region, we received our first at-large bid to compete at the 2010 NCAA D-III National Women's Golf Championship.

Setting the bar high, seeing ourselves reach our goal, believing in it, and then taking action and executing our plan, is how we achieved the dream. "Taking action is what clears the path," says spiritual guru and author, Gabrielle Bernstein.[2]

When you have a clear vision for what you want, and you are willing to put in the work, it's super exciting—but never an actual surprise—when you get there. We all knew that very first year that it was possible to get to a National Championship and that we would get there—that is *why* we arrived. But we could not rush building the attributes that got us there: visualization, consistency, and hard work.

Mental Toughness Training Tip:

Set a goal and visualize yourself achieving it. Critical!

In today's sports world, bringing in new players to replace existing ones is the norm, especially with the transfer portal now so prevalent and available to athletes and coaches. As a result, players no longer have to be all that loyal, and coaches have a place to go to find solid competitors. This approach can work, and no doubt help improve teams faster, but I still believe the culture and chemistry of the players are what dictate success.

Team chemistry is vital to winning championships and that is where development is essential. Many programs glide in and out of the Top 10 national rankings year after year because players graduate or transfer, and new recruits aren't yet aligned with a disciplined and winning team culture.

I understand that coaches feel the pressure for instant success and thus, prioritize recruiting over development. The key is doing both with the recruiting of players who fit your culture and staying patient with development.

PATIENCE RULES

Our team has a bamboo tradition, where each year our new players receive a bamboo plant to represent the patience it takes to grow and become successful. In his book *Water the Bamboo*, Greg Bell, motivational speaker and University of Oregon alum, writes about how giant timber bamboo farmers can water and water and see no growth for long periods of time. Yet, the farmers will keep watering because they know that one day, their bamboo will shoot up, sometimes as much as "90 feet in 60 days—that's a foot and a half a day!"[3] Bell explains in his book. The same is true for top athletes. You might not immediately see new growth, but if you stay persistent and consistent, put in the work, then BAM, you take off!

> *Mental Toughness Training Tip:*
>
> *Patience is a superpower for success. Allow yourself time to get to your destiny!*

Which brings me to one player who didn't make it into the five-person team lineup for two years—but by her junior year, she became a superstar. The second time she played in the line-up, she won the entire event receiving medalist honors!

What did it take? How did she do it?

She was like the bamboo farmers. She was patient. She was confident in positive outcomes. She worked really hard. The player tried to qualify but missed the mark by just a few strokes. But she went back to work. She kept a positive attitude. She did not blame me or her parents. She did not blame her teammates, her boyfriend, or anything. She just kept at it. She improved on areas of her game that weren't as strong and even on the components that were already her strengths. She listened, accepted her mistakes, learned from them, and grew some more.

Our player wrote affirmations. She visualized. She saw herself becoming a winning player. Ultimately, she broke down the resistance that was holding her back and her magic arrived—with fireworks!

It's absolutely a coach's dream when an athlete reaches that special place you know is there, but never quite know if your player can find it. She found it—with mastery.

Many players talk to me about needing or wanting their success to happen immediately. Like right now. Tomorrow at the latest. I always know it's going to take that player longer. You have to put in the work and then allow it to happen. Sometimes you see little to no advancement and just have to believe it's coming.

In the end, her winning talent was inherent, but it was her inner game and mental strength that were limiting her. When she hit an errant shot, she was always way too hard on herself. Granted, she was a perfectionist like many top student-athletes. It's difficult to let go of the mistakes and focus on the process. The misses can discourage and frustrate us—and make us wonder if the hard work is ever going to pay off.

Eventually, our superstar realized she was getting in her own way and had to make a change. So, she did.

A favorite quote on resistance is from Steven Pressfield's *The War of Art* which is more about what it takes to be a great writer, but I think it applies well to sports, too. "Resistance is most powerful at the finish line."[4]

I tell myself and the team that all the time. Many times, we want to quit before the magic happens because we can't wait any longer and we give up. We have to realize that we are so much closer than we think and keep pushing on.

Mental Toughness Training Tip:

The journey is about patience and persistence. Stay on the marathon journey to greatness. It's in you. Many give up before the magic truly sparks. Know it's there and keep advancing. One percent better each day does add up to that winning percentage eventually.

STOP, LOOK, LISTEN TO YOUR HEART

I am always reading, watching, observing, learning, and exploring new ways to improve as a coach. While attending the LPGA Portland Classic, I was fortunate to have an opportunity to talk to some LPGA rookies who were on Duke University's National Championship team in 2007. Duke had a four-season winning streak between 2004 and 2007. I asked these players about the one thing I should be doing as a coach to lead our team to the next level. I thought for sure they would tell me short game, short game, short game, since 60 percent of the game is won from 100 yards in. Instead, they told me to focus on building a strong culture. They said that culture is the essential key to long-term success. They did add, but short game, short game short game helps, too!

The Duke Champions said they could not have done it without the incredible support from each other and the coach. Their commitment, dedication—and loyalty—were not just for themselves, but for each other and their university.

Their final nugget of advice? *Body language is everything.* If you are a championship team, then you act like a championship team always. You walk like it, talk like it, dress like it and mean it, even before you win a championship. Then when you are playing your sport, you show that same confidence no matter what. They said at no point, could a player look across a fairway and tell how another teammate was playing. This was also incorporated in our program from very early on, but we are always learning how to be even better.

Mental Toughness Training Tip:

Act like a champion before you are champion. You can't be a champion until you see yourself being a champion.

A lot of the drive I had for building a new program was that I was super fortunate to have a University President who was supportive of athletics—and me. That advocacy played (and still plays) a crucial role in what I would accomplish. During my first coaching experience at another college across town, the president made it quite clear that he did not care for athletics. In fact, he actually told one of our players that she should have stayed with music rather than golf. Teams struggle to build a program without a supportive administration and community of encouragement.

I definitely had allies at my new job, and it felt so good. I also had tremendous support from three outstanding coaches (women's basketball, baseball and track & field) at the school who either had already won a National Championship or were headed to win one in a few years. Those coaches offered incredible influential tips that helped me understand what it was going to take to be successful. Mentors are so important!

How do we arrive at The Show—how do we get there? With the help of my mentors, I realized I needed to slow my roll and derive a methodical, more consistent, and focused process rather than try to launch a rocket. Consistency is one of my secret weapons. You have to take disciplined steps toward improvement each day to achieve your goal. That part was not easy but paid off.

We started with nothing, but we acted and worked like we were champions from the get-go. And sure enough, in just four years, we arrived at the 2010 National Championship for the first time! Yes, indeed. Girls can win. Grit pays dividends.

Mental Toughness Training Tip:

Work on getting one percent better each day. We may not always feel like doing the work but being consistent each day brings bigger improvement and success.

Special Nugget for When Girls Win!

When Girls Win, we know that team culture, chemistry and patience are critical to success. Mutual support and encouragement are also part of the winning formula. We avoid the rush to get there and understand that slow and steady always wins the race!

WALKING ON SUNSHINE—AND DON'T IT FEEL GOOD

I just skated for the FUN of it!

–Sarah Hughes, 2002 Olympic Gold Medalist, U.S. figure skating

One night I was at home quietly reading upstairs when my husband eagerly called me down to our family room to watch something on TV. I thought for sure something was wrong, as he emphatically yelled several times, which was unlike him. I hurried downstairs, expecting to see a disastrous *Breaking News* banner, but instead, I was surprised to see a young woman sitting at a big green table with several men playing cards. Huh? I was irritated! "You called me to rush down here to watch poker with you?"

Turns out it was the World Series of Poker Tournament of Champions on ESPN and Annie Duke was the lone female in the competition. Annie was playing for a chance to win $2 million. "Just watch her— you can't tell if she has a great hand or nothing at all," my hubby mused.

I told him I really didn't care to watch poker, nor did I really know much about the game. I turned to leave the room when he gently urged me again, "Please, just watch her for a few minutes. I promise you it will be worth your time."

I stayed only because he was so adamant, and suddenly found myself drawn into the game as well. Here was this self-assured woman sitting at this male-dominated high-stakes poker table—poised, calm and apparently winning.

She was casually chatting with the guys and even acted like she didn't care if she won or lost. She simply looked like she was having a lot of fun, thriving in the moment. No one tuning in would have known that $2 million was at stake—except for the announcer reminding us every few minutes.

"If you make it obvious what cards you are holding, you will have a tougher time winning in the future," explained my husband. His statement caught me a little off-guard. Am I *that* obvious?!' He paused. I knew the answer then was yes.

What he was trying to tell me, in his own creative way, was I might need to change my strategy when dealing with the other male coaches. If I showed strong negative emotion—like anger or frustration—about issues I was trying to change to improve our team, the guys would throw me off balance and vote against me. Then I would have to work that much harder to hurdle the traditional barriers that were interfering with our team and our overall goals. There was constant resistance from my male peers when I wanted to make changes like allowing more players into our Northwest Conference tournaments. Our Conference was seeing growth, and I wanted to see more opportunities for women. There was no reason not to add another tee time or two to our events.

I am a proponent of offering opportunities. I always like to travel with an individual to give that person experience, and I always appreciate

D-I and D-II teams giving D-III teams an opportunity to play in bigger tournaments. Our mission as coaches should be to grow the game and not just make it easier on ourselves.

While I was not into poker, this scenario was a wake-up call for me. Sometimes we need to hear and see things several different ways to really understand the call-to-action—not unlike seeing a product advertised several times before making the purchase. Finally, I got the message. I'd been tipping my hand. Change was necessary.

ODE TO JOY

I began to understand the strategy as I watched Annie closely. No one could tell if she was bluffing or had a handful of aces. And she was having a blast! Yes indeed, I had to figure out a way to behave more like this talented female poker player. I needed to subdue those negative emotions around the other coaches. Instead, I needed to embrace and exude joy in order to move the needle. I vowed I would enjoy the journey even when I was met with resistance, and I'd get off the negative train if my male peers voted me down.

Same thing with my players. I had to keep them from boarding that downer bandwagon as well. I needed to guide them toward releasing expectations and remind them why they began playing their sport in the first place. It is usually joy that attracts a player to the sport. Joy draws a person into wanting to play, excel and progress. Sometimes that spark can dim as pressure and stress mount and the stakes get higher.

Mental Toughness Training Tip:

Winning comes from finding your way to the highest vibration which is joy! Joy in your hard work. Joy in your progress. Joy in striving toward a bigger goal. Joy in the special moments along the way. Joy in the opportunity to play or coach a sport that you love! The winning is in the joy. It's the gift for getting to do what you love and the freedom to be in a state where fear does not exist. It does not mean you'll always earn a trophy, but if you continue in a high vibe mindset—success will find you.

Note: Annie Duke got the job done and knocked out eight of the best poker players in the world to win the World Poker Championship. She was the first woman to ever do so.

Mental Toughness Training Tip:

Understand that we all have emotions, but if you can learn to observe the negative ones and continue to focus on joy and doing what you love, you will find more positivity and success. Plus, you will create a stronger edge over the competition.

"Don't let catching fish get in the way of your joy of fishing!" says my fave marketing guru Seth Godin.[1]

Remember joy is the major *why* for putting in the work and getting to the next level. Joy is the foundation for mastering the process it requires to grow.

I frequently tell my players the story about Olympic figure skater, Sarah Hughes. I've repeated it so many times they know it by heart. Yet, they still want to hear the story again as a reminder.

Michelle Kwan was the overwhelming favorite in the 2002 Winter Olympics in Salt Lake City. She seemed obsessed with winning Gold and even wore an all gold-colored skating outfit in the finals. Michelle had failed at the Gold Medal four years earlier and was under an enormous pressure to win.

Meanwhile, Sarah Hughes seemed to come out of nowhere, cruising out on the ice like a happy-go-lucky girl joyfully zipping around without a care in the world. My sister, who was always into the Winter Olympics figure skating events like me, called me and asked, "Have you heard of this skater?" I had not, but we both felt like we were almost friends with Michelle Kwan, as we had read and heard so much about her.

Sarah finished fourth in the short program while Michelle finished first so everyone assumed that Michelle's gold dress would indeed match her Olympic medal. Sarah seemed to have very little chance of winning but didn't seem to care. She told announcers that she was skating to have fun and enjoy the experience. She skated brilliantly in the long program and scored close to a perfect performance as she hit all her jumps.

Meanwhile Michelle missed jumps and the mistakes mounted as she seemed to be trying too hard to win. Sure enough, Sarah scored Gold and afterwards acknowledged how much joy she felt just being on the ice. "It's really ironic that I won, because that's not the goal I had when I went out to skate," she admitted.

CAN'T STOP THE FEELING

Not only is joy in what you are doing fundamental to winning but exuding a joyful and positive energy is key to your performance as well.

One of our players shot a personal best, breaking 70 for the first time at a tournament in Victoria BC—mostly because of the fun-loving and the joyful energy she radiated. We had not experienced a road trip via bus with our men's golf team before, nor had we ever traveled to Canada, so it was a new adventure for everyone. I was the only one onboard who had visited Victoria before, so when we arrived into the harbor by ferry, I was excited to play tour guide and share the landmarks.

As I was pointing over to the beautiful Parliament building, everyone started laughing and screaming. I was completely clueless and thought they really loved Victoria more than I thought they would! When I looked a little closer, I saw hundreds of people splashed in fake blood participating in a zombie walk in the park next to the Parliament building. None of us had ever seen this zombie theater in action—an unforgettable scene on our Canadian journey! Our bus was still full of laughter when we stopped at the course to get in some practice time. Everyone was smiling and pumped up to put in the work. Incredible energy and excitement remained in the air even after our long day of travel.

Did our player shoot a personal best because she witnessed a zombie walk? Absolutely not. But the entertainment created such positive energy as she embraced every minute of our journey that it carried over to the golf course. Exhilarating feelings create more exhilarating feelings. And vice a versa. If you are worried about your play and dreading a poor performance—you will attract what you are worried about.

After the round, I asked the star player if she felt anything different before her round that day. She had struggled with her game a few weeks prior and suddenly was finding her magic on the course. She told me that it just felt so easy that day because she "felt so much joy around in her heart." She was having fun with her teammates, and she couldn't wait to tell her parents about the experience. She said she finally felt the freedom to let go and play the game she loved rather than being trapped by focusing on a winning score.

She probably would have shot even lower, but she realized with a few holes left just how well she was doing. Once she became conscious of her low score and started counting strokes, she lost some of her natural flow state. Still, she was able to stay in her zone enough to shoot 3 under par and finish in a tie for 2nd place against some fierce competition.

Special Nugget for When Girls Win!

When Girls Win, we no longer seek ways to prove ourselves to anyone. We are true to ourselves and find joy following our passion. When we struggle with negative emotions, we know how to quickly get back to a higher vibration. We know that higher vibrational energy—Joy!—guarantees our best outcome.

With increased self-awareness, we learn to let go of things we can't control and stay in our own joyful place. We navigate roadblocks—even the political ones—and realize our power is founded in our joy and passion for the game.

9

PICK UP THE PIECES

The only person who can stop you from reaching your goals is you.

–Jackie Joyner Kersee, Three-time Olympic Gold Medalist U.S. Track & Field

I want to take you back to our first National Championship bid and the incredible number of lessons I learned.

Just four years after the launch of our new collegiate golf program, we received our first bid to play in the NCAA D-III National Championship. What was interesting is that although we finished as co-champions in our Conference, the other team received the Automatic Qualifier (AQ) while we had to wait to get a bid. Our Conference has three championship events—the first two counting 25 percent and the final counting 50 percent. Our team won the first two events by over 30 strokes and then lost the last one by four strokes. Unfortunately, the tiebreaker for Nationals was the team that won the last match. So even though we were over 20 strokes ahead of the other team in the three conference events, we were left waiting.

I was naïve about the bid selection system at the time and was surprised when I heard from many that we most likely would not get a bid. Others in college athletics had told me it was political and not to get our hopes up because a Northwest school is rarely selected. Apparently, our team shocked a lot of people when our invitation arrived, and we were on our way to our first Big Show.

Mental Toughness Training Tip:

A reminder to DREAM BIG! Make your goal to WIN. Never to just show up.

This selection bid meant we would be traveling to none other than Howey-in-the-Hills to go after our ultimate dream: winning the National Championship! Howey-in-the-Hills? The name may sound a little like a village in the Cotswolds, England, that features towns such as Stow-on-the-Wold or Bourton-on-the-Water. One quick Google search told me Howey is a little town of about 1,000 people right smack in the center of Florida, the Sunshine State.

The name of the town is fitting, as we discover that the only hills in this sea-level state are located directly in the middle of the golf course we'll be playing. Note: The NCAA National Championship sites change locations most years in D-III based on a bidding process, but Howey has been an ongoing popular one for the NCAA Championships.

About a week before the Championship, the pairings for the first two days were released for the four-day, 72-hole tournament. We would be paired with the top two teams in the nation. Not sure how the NCAA scoring company, Golfstat, came up with *that* calculation, which landed us in the toughest pairing right out of the gate, but there we were. Why not start at the top for our first visit to the Natties?

Both those top schools had strong reputations, especially since one of them had won the NCAA National Women's Championship (D-III) over ten years in a row. No doubt we were the underdogs being paired with the best two teams right out of the gate. The thought of competing with the best in the country was a little nerve-racking at first, but I knew my job was to have our team ready to go, so that's what I focused on.

Mental Toughness Training Tip:

Preparation is everything. Be prepared for all the challenges you will face. Have a plan before arriving at your competition takes diligence but will help you feel ready when you get there and separate you from the competition. The more you can see yourself in the moment before you are actually in it, the better prepared you will be.

After landing in Orlando, we grab our van to continue our journey to Howey—a little over an hour from the airport. "Aruba, Jamaica, oh I want to take ya, to Bermuda, Bahama, come on pretty Mama" is blasting from our van windows and we're feeling that Beach Boys vibe cruising along under the bright blue, sunny Florida skies. After all, this special place is home to Disney, Epcot, Sea World, gorgeous beaches, and beautiful golf courses—a playground of fun many of us have never experienced before.

The road trip from the airport to the resort seems to drag on for much longer than we expect as we take a bunch of "we're almost there" rally videos –but still find ourselves waiting. Finally, we spot the big "M.I." on the gate of the Mission Inn Resort. I'm just hoping the letters don't stand for *Mission Impossible,* which I had overheard a few of my colleagues call it jokingly—or maybe not so jokingly!

Regardless, we are feeling mission-ready to attack the course as we see the NCAA flag and all our collegiate flags flying high along the palm-tree lined road leading up to the resort's main entrance. We are proud to see our school flag and slow down to take pictures from the van windows. Almost on cue, an alligator peaks out from behind a small waterfall at the entrance as if to greet us! The energy level in the van spikes to a new high. The thrill of competing in this big event is really happening. Are we ready?

UP ON A TIGHTROPE

Day one arrives and despite all my meditation, affirmations, positive mindset, journaling, and mental preparation (and I must admit, a few Tums!), the nerves are kicking in, Big Time. I keep thinking, *Nerves are good, right?* As I head to the van, I give myself the same pep talk I gave the team the night before, but still, my stomach is tied up in knots.

Our team enthusiastically loads up the van to drive the barely three minutes over to the golf course. One player asked to DJ our pre-tournament music and starts her first selection. The minute we roll out of the parking lot "The Final Countdown" by the group Europe began to play over the van speakers. I am sure she had great intentions, but the song elicited visions of the final farewell and then maybe not coming back at all.

Yikes! In less than 30 seconds, the van vibe slips from excitement to dread. We are living the Final Countdown and I can't help but wonder if things will "ever be the same again"—the words from the song now raging in my head.

Just as we pull into the parking lot, the next song up, "Under Pressure" begins, and I feel an intense adrenaline rush. I immediately pull out the aux cord. I turn around in my seat to face the team and all I can see is fear on their faces. I quickly thank our player for the tunes as she definitely nailed it as far as how we were all feeling with the countdown and all. Unfortunately, it created an unwelcome intensity I had not felt with the team before. I swallow hard and stick with our usual routine in the van, but I know if I try to rally the team with something that even I am not believing at the time, the players will not believe it either.

In that moment, fear seems to have captured us all.

I take some deep breaths and run through our goal for the day, which is routine for all our tournaments. A few smiles emerge as comfort with our usual routine begins to replace the fear. Some relief sets in for me as well. I slowly return to believing we can do it and get into pep talk mode. We talk about what's for lunch and the food distraction seems to replace the uneasy tension in the air. But in reality, I am thinking, *how can I figure out a way to get that song out of my head?*

Note to self, lock into a singalong song next time, like *Sweet Caroline* to be sure to keep an uplifting vibe. You can't go wrong with Neil Diamond.

Our players slowly make their way out of the van, change into their golf shoes, apply a not-so-pleasant-smelling concoction of sunscreen mixed with bug spray, and prepare their bags with snacks and water. I pull on our team duffel bag that is stuffed with snacks and squished in between the two front seats and maneuver it out of the van and onto my shoulder. Then, I walk with our team of five over to the main practice green. As we start to see the other teams arriving, the excitement level continues to escalate.

A few of our players head to the range to warm up while I stay back on the putting green with the others who will be teeing off a little later. I keep trying to get into that "it's just another tournament mode," but it's difficult when there are huge team flags flying high next to the putting green and an enormous blue and white NCAA National Championship banner painted on a grassy hillside next to the green. I do my best to look composed even though my heart won't stop pounding. I pause to tell one player that her practice shots look good hoping that I am possibly adding that last bit of confidence before the round.

Players take turns going over to the range to hit balls. Everyone is quietly going about their business with their own teams and the only sound heard around the enormous green is ice swishing back and forth in coolers strapped to the back of coaches' carts as they are passing by.

As cool as I hope to be appearing on the outside, my unsettled nerves are back on the loose as we become surrounded by more and more players and coaches on the putting green. We arrived early, but now all the teams going off around our time on both holes 1 and 10 are arriving, so the practice green becomes packed. A mixture of anxiety and tension engulfs me, along with the fragrant smell of gardenias, mixed with a splash of Banana Boat suntan lotion. I focus on the smell to get back in the moment and I slowly feel my tense shoulders start to lower.

TAKE A BREATH

I know you may be thinking, *Why is this coach who is supposed to be so mentally tough and is teaching us mental toughness so nervous right now?* Well, when you are first placed in that Big Moment Experience that you have never been in before, it's amazing how your mind can race in the wrong direction and old habits pop up out of nowhere.

My thoughts start down the *what if* path. What if we don't play well? What if our team looks bad? What if we are way overrated? What if we finish last? This coach is feeling some of the same nervous energy that the players are feeling. I tell myself what I am telling the team to do: Stay in the moment! Focusing on the *what ifs* and the potential outcome, is highly ineffective and will only hurt your chances. Locking into the present moment and embracing the experience—albeit pressure-filled—is where peace and joy exist.

> *Mental Toughness Training Tip:*
>
> *In tension-filled situations, use your senses as much as possible to stay in the now. It may sound strange, but it works. Focusing on your feet on the ground or the smells in the air or the breeze on your cheeks keeps you away from worry and anxiety about the future outcome or past mistakes you made.*

As I approach the first tee, I see the yellow ropes securing the area inside the tee box that only players and coaches can enter. I notice the first tee announcer in charge of starting players off is dressed in a nice sports jacket with a tie. This is not a normal occurrence during the season, so the formality of it all signals us that we have arrived and it's now go-time on the Big Stage, whether we are ready or not.

The announcer sees me and walks over to introduce himself. Then he informs me that I need to sign in as the coach and put my coach's bracelet on before the first player in our first group tees off. He tells me that wearing the colorful NCAA bracelet means that for the next six or so hours, I am identified by the NCAA as the only coach—the only person—allowed to talk to my players while they are competing. I think to myself, *wow, even Sister J.R. can't save me now!* In fact, where is that positive self-talk when I need it? I tell myself to just keep breathing, smell the mixed fragrances in the air, and look up at the one puff of a cloud drifting by in the expansive bright blue sky.

Mental Toughness Training Tip:

> *Mental toughness training is an ongoing process. Many times, we must go back to our toolbox for help to find what works best for us.*

I rush back over to my cart to grab some suntan lotion and apply one last slather of sunscreen to my arms as they are already heating up in the brilliant sunshine. I check my watch and see that it's not even noon yet, and I can't believe how scorching hot it is already. I clean my shades one last time, put them back on under my visor and walk over to introduce myself to the two top coaches who have just arrived. Our team will be paired with their two teams for the first two 18-hole rounds the first two days and then re-paired by scores for the final two rounds. These top coaches are both men, but I am confident, prepared, and ready.

At first, I feel a little intimidated as the coaches remain focused and intense while both giving me rather firm handshakes. Then, I give myself a little affirmational boost by telling myself, "Okay, game on, let's go!"

I am super excited and take some deep breaths to calm myself down as I try to concentrate on my own players. We are off the first tee in three-some pairings with our #5 players going off first, then 4th, 3rd, and 2nd, finishing with the #1 player. I don't like to label these players by number, as our players are all good, but that's just how a golf line-up works. The ending team score is the best four out of five players each day for the four days.

Our first few players all miss their drives to the right off the 1st hole but manage to recover with their second shots. I take another deep breath and drive down the first fairway in my cart to follow my coaching game plan for the day.

Since the first hole's putting green is close to the 2nd hole tee box, my plan is to drive up and park by the 2nd tee box. I can then position myself between the green on the 1st hole and the tee box on the 2nd hole to go back and forth between our five groups as each one finishes on number one and heads over to number two. My plan is to keep driving up about three holes at a time to stay up with the front of the pack as our players come through one-by-one on these difficult starting holes.

I observe the action mostly on the sidelines unless it looks like a player needs help or a boost of confidence. I want them to be free from thoughts and to just play their games. My nerves are subsiding a little now as I get settled into my usual routine, and I confidently smile at some family members of my players. I'm doing my best to feel like I belong on this national stage.

Mental Toughness Training Tip:

Your routine keeps you in the moment and works as your safety net. It is calming to your mind to do it the same way each time and reduces anxiety and stress. Lock into your successful routines whether you are a coach or a player. Also remember besides looking like you belong, FEEL like you belong. You have earned it.

YOU VS. YOU

At this point, I am not noticing anything different about the two other coaches' golf carts which are parked next to mine on the cart path by the 2nd tee box, but then I clue in that they are pointed in the opposite direction of mine. Suddenly, as our last player taps in her putt on the 1st hole, both coaches start sprinting toward their carts, jump in and take off in the opposite direction of the 2nd hole. I am left standing there watching them and now in a panic wondering what they know that I don't know.

The coaches are headed toward the 16th hole! Huh? I am so confused on why their plan is so different from mine. I start thinking there must be something they know that I do not know. I quickly confirm the yardage for our final player teeing off on the 2nd hole, wait briefly for her to hit, and then I can't stand it any longer. I rush over to my cart almost like I'm on autopilot, jump in, swing it around in the opposite direction and start speeding after the other coaches.

Yes, I must admit, in an instant, the NCAA National Women's Golf Championship turned into a bit of an unexpected NASCAR race across the rolling fairways of Howey. The driving course was complete with hairpin turns around several large bunkers and sprawling water lily ponds where the alligators lurk.

The enormous shrubbery and palm trees are now just a blur as my golf cart pedal is slammed to the floor and we bolt along at maximum speed. I am compelled to make sure that the other coaches have not outsmarted me in any way. They clearly have a different plan than mine, and I need to find out what it is to make sure I am not putting our team at any disadvantage.

I knew these coaches were headed to a different hole than I had planned, but I wasn't quite sure why they were taking this cross-country route from the back nine. They knew the course way better than I did as both had played it at previous championships. I continue to worry they know something I don't know.

KEEP YOUR COOL

Before I can continue the story, I have to explain about the need to keep cool in the heat—physically and figuratively speaking as well! I never thought about needing a cooler on my coach's golf cart in Florida until I noticed that all the other coaches had them during our practice round the previous day. No one told me to bring a cooler. The NCAA was providing water at various stations along the course, but the ability to give your players immediate access to ice and water is critically important in the heat where ultra-high humidity is adding to the heat index. Our team from Oregon experienced a 40-degree jump in temperature in just a five-hour plane ride and hydration is a key component for performance for any athlete.

When I realized that a cooler was essential, that night I drove out to a nearby store to find something that might work. The best I could do was pick up a small, cheap Styrofoam cooler as the size choices were so limited. I swear I am normally a very ecological Oregonian, but once again low price plays a big role in collegiate athletics.

When we arrive at the course the next day, we put our handy little cooler full of ice, water, and Gatorade on the back of my coach's cart. However, when I floored the cart backwards to turn around and follow the other two coaches, I accidentally hit a huge bump next to the cart path—and as fate would have it, chunks of our Styrofoam cooler broke off and spewed all over the grass. As I was speeding along, I heard a noise, looked behind me to see my cracked cooler blowing up behind me. I whipped around and cruised back to responsibly pick up the broken foam, then quickly took off to see if I could still spot the other coaches' carts.

My heart was racing along with the cart as reality was setting in that I had just abandoned the team and my own game plan to figure out what the heck was happening!

Luckily, I caught sight of two carts through the trees zipping across the 6th hole about two fairways over, so I did a little off-roading to get there faster. Whoops—now more Styrofoam pieces are flying. I stop again, pick up the pieces, and keep on tracking down the 6th hole.

Since this was my first time at the tournament, and as much as I had studied the holes on the course, I didn't know the layout all that well yet or the shortcuts. Clearly, this was a shortcut. I hate to admit this, but I honestly had no idea what exact hole these two coaches were headed toward. I knew it had to be a short-cut, but this was a new track for me. What *did* these guys know anyway!?

As I closed the gap, I could see the other coaches' carts parked at the bottom of the hill next to the raised 5th green that sits at the top of a big incline. The putting green has a few large tiers to it and is one of the widest greens on the course. I notice the coaches walking around the green where our first group of players are now putting. I never guessed that our first group of players would be that quickly down the 5th hole and on that green already. They were playing much faster than I had anticipated. The other coaches must have looked at the hole-by-hole online updates while I was nervously trying to look calm and smiling and waving at everyone on the 1st hole.

I'm suddenly annoyed. I sacrificed my brand-new Styrofoam cooler to land here? What is this strategy all about? Then I realize that due to the dramatic slope and undulation of the green, these coaches had chosen this spot to help their players get a better read on their putts and basically try to help prevent them from three-putting.

I nonchalantly hop out of my cart like this was my plan all along and head over to the green where my player is waiting her turn to putt. I whisper to her quietly, "Do you need a read?" I had never helped her read putts before, so she looked at me completely confused but then offered a nervous giggle and said she was fine.

My competitive drive—figuratively and literally—got the best of me. It was absolutely silly that I put myself in a ridiculous cross-course chase due to my absurd fear of not knowing something they did. Clearly, I should have trusted and followed my own game plan.

Why was I not trusting myself and my coaching skills? It was Me v. Me. Ouch.

While the other player is putting, I open my phone to check the online scoreboard and see that one of our players took a triple bogey—three over par–on the 3rd hole and another a double bogey on the 4th hole. Not good scores if you don't know much about golf. Our team had already run into some early problems, and I completely missed it all because I didn't trust myself or my plan.

LESSON LEARNED. THE HARD WAY.

I could have been there for our players, or at least for one of them— who I later found out had hit into a trouble area and made a costly decision under pressure. I know that you can't be everywhere as a golf coach when you have five players spread out over three or four holes, but your job is to make the best choices you can. In the end, I learned my lesson that our own team plan would have been the best direction for us and there was no reason to suddenly change it.

Additional word to the wise: Bring a non-Styrofoam cooler next time!

> *Mental Toughness Training Tip:*
>
> *You do you! PERIOD! Trust your own game. If you have one eye on someone else's game, how can you truly focus on your own? TRUST YOURSELF. Be YOU. It's **you versus you** out there and no one else.*

"COMPARISON IS THE THIEF OF JOY." –TEDDY ROOSEVELT

Athletes need to stick to their game plan as well. What was interesting is that not only did I get caught in the mistake of comparison, but I realized just how much comparing and judging goes on between the players as well. It's important to stomp that out quickly. If my player felt like she was beating the other players in her group, she felt good about her game and played better. If she was not winning in her group, she felt bad, got down on herself quickly and did not play to her potential for the whole day.

I cleared my head and got back on track with my game plan as our players were moving to the back nine just as one of my players approached me in between shots on the 11th hole quite shaken, tears welling in her eyes. She told me that one of the competitors in her pairing was on fire. So, this girl-on-fire was creating anxiety for my player, and directly derailing her performance. I encouraged her to focus on her own game—a really hard feat when the other player was beating her so badly shooting birdie after birdie.

My player's panic was escalating as she became more concerned with her opponent's performance and more worried about a poor outcome. She had become obsessed with what she *could not* control and lost sight of what she *could* control. As a result, the player lost confidence in her own game, and while she recognized that, the downward spiral had begun, and she couldn't stop it. How do you snap out of the free fall?

Mental Toughness Training Tip:

As you get to a higher level and the competition becomes even more fierce, your mental toughness training and commitment must continue to get stronger. You have to learn to block out what others are doing and understand that your competitors are going to play great as well. You must learn to ride their momentum and view it positively like "If they play well, I can, too." This more positive outlook keeps your emotions intact. Basically, the goal is always to focus on what you can control—YOU and YOUR MINDSET. No comparing yourself or your game with anyone else —or you will get distracted and end up in worse shape.

OWN YOUR GAME AND TRUST IN YOURSELF.

The next day, a competitor who was playing with our #1 player scored a hole-in-one on the 8th hole, a short par three. It was our

17th hole in the tournament—as we went off the backside first. Our player knew she was staying strong and ahead of the players in the group going into the last few holes, even as her competitors were playing well. She had not hit her tee shot yet, and after witnessing the hole-in-one, she turned to me completely frustrated and asked in an agitated tone, "Now what am I supposed to do?"

I could see her wildly competitive spirit as she knew the odds of following an ace with another ace was nearly impossible. I told her to start by congratulating the other player and then to go hit a great shot herself! A truly talented player, she was also caught in the comparison game.

Mental Toughness Training Tip:

Reminder, elite competitors know what they can control and let go of the things they can NOT control.

"THE ONLY THING WE HAVE TO FEAR IS FEAR ITSELF."–FRANKLIN D. ROOSEVELT

This first trip to Nationals taught our team and me a lot about comparing and how much it can negatively impact performance. It's like judging. You can't put any energy into it, as it will only diminish your own winning vibe. I was comparing myself out there to the other coaches and some of my players were comparing themselves to their competition instead of just trusting ourselves, our games, and our plan. The internal fear we created was taunting us that we weren't good enough. But we *are* good enough—that's why we made it to the Natties!

Remember, *FEAR is an acronym for* **F**alse **E**vidence **A**ppearing **R**eal. Fear feeds off ego and can misrepresent what is real. If you remember what fear actually is in the sports arena, you can shake it off and resume trusting yourself. Both the team and I succumbed to fear. We needed to acknowledge that and release it quicker. Our egos wanted to prove themselves and demonstrate our worthiness in being there on the national stage.

Many people are too afraid to be honest with themselves, look inward and identify how they can improve next time. I am not scared to be vulnerable, telling the silly race story. And I have to admit that I abandoned my coaching game plan for a short period of time because I was fearful my strategy and I were not good enough. I second-guessed myself. But I grew so much from the experience that it helped me understand myself better and how I needed to be true to myself and expertise in order to be a better coach.

Simply put, I don't recommend chasing other coaches' golf carts!

I realized it was ridiculous for me to worry about not measuring up— not being as good as the male coaches. I needed to be a role model for my players when they bought into their own comparison games. I had to show my strength and exhibit confidence in myself and in our team. If I was throwing our game plan out the window by the 2nd hole, then I had one eye on the competition and definitely less focus on our team.

Our players also learned that "comparison is a thief" and wreaks havoc on peak performance.

"DWELL IN POSSIBILITY." –EMILY DICKINSON

A magic staircase to the top of the podium does not exist. The path to getting there is a constant learning and growing process. We all experience setbacks and failures as an important part of the journey. It's inevitably what keeps us going and on track to mastery. Following a mastery mindset as opposed to a fixed mindset is a big lesson. We want to keep growing and testing ourselves and learning more in order to see how far we can go. That's how we master our craft.

Another nugget I've learned is that we must embrace all of our experiences with gratitude and feed our subconscious minds good vibes, not useless negative ones. Gratitude and learning from our mistakes will better prepare us for next time. If we stew over failures, we are only feeding those negative thoughts to our subconscious mind.

Always remember that your subconscious mind wants to give you what it thinks you want. So, if we tell ourselves, "I am a confident player—or coach—and I trust my preparation, I trust my plan," our mind will then honor us as a confident and competent player. We can trust ourselves and our preparation. Confidence is something you must practice long before you get to the Championship!

We finished our first Championship appearance in eighth place, despite all the nerves, fear, and crazy mistakes. It was the first time that any golf team in our Northwest Conference—men or women—had finished in the top 10 on the biggest stage, which made it even more special.

Mental Toughness Training Tip:

Consistency wins. Leave overnight success to Fed Ex. Keep learning and growing each and every day. One percent improvement each day is better than trying for five percent on one day and zero the next. Trying to go for too much at once can wear you down over time. Consistency brings results.

As Zen Monk Shunryu Suzuki said, "In the beginner's mind, there are many possibilities, but in the expert's mind, there are few."[1] Always stay OPEN to the possibilities.

Special Nugget for When Girls Win!

When Girls Win, we believe in ourselves to the fullest. We are free of fear and doubt, and we own who we are and what we have worked hard to achieve. Our confidence shines as we go after our goals knowing we are ready. We believe in who we are and our gifts and intelligence. Even in big moments, we remember to be ourselves and no one else!

SUPER TROUPER LIGHTS ARE GONNA FIND ME

Mental will is a muscle that needs exercise,
just like the muscles of the body.

–Lynn Jennings, Top American long-distance runner
Olympic Bronze Medal in 10,000 meters US Track & Field

E arly in my coaching career, our team was fortunate to have PGA tour professional Peter Jacobsen visit one of our team practices. I will never forget Peter's words of wisdom. One of our players was hitting bunker shots, and when he walked over, she self-consciously told him not to watch as it made her too nervous. He smiled and jumped into the bunker to show her how to hit the shot and said, "What? Don't you know when you play golf, you are in the entertainment business? It may look like a sport, but you are here to put on a great show!"

Everyone laughed, but what he said was powerful. We work diligently on our craft, rehearse, and then it's *show time*. If we are lucky and talented enough, we will attract an audience. In the end, the ultimate adrenaline rush as an athlete is being that player who nails the shot at the end of the game to bring it on home in front of our fans.

Mental Toughness Training Tip:

Growth happens when you step outside your comfort zone. Many athletes know this but forget to practice it regularly or resist it because it's too uncomfortable. Learning to be comfortable when you are uncomfortable will help you grow and master the game.

Stepping outside your comfort zone means working on shots or areas of your game that make you feel uncomfortable. It can be frustrating. You will struggle some, but that is when you grow the most. It's called reaching.

In *The Little Book of Talent,* author Daniel Coyle discusses visiting elite world-class athletes and musicians across the globe to see what set them apart. He described the elite as those more willing to *reach* while practicing.[1] He learned that exploring one's potential while rehearsing is the big separator between average and elite players. Those who are unafraid to push themselves to develop a new skill or improve in a weaker area experience more growth and outshine others. That's the key. If you keep doing the same old thing, you will keep getting the same old results. My coaching philosophy is to mix it up, try new things and seek new ways to keep my players reaching—exploring potential.

CHANGE IT

Key to improving? If you don't like putting from the fringe off the green, work on it. If you dislike hitting longer chip shots, practice them. If you dread the 40-yard pitch shot, just do it. If you fear long bunker shots, rehearse, and rehearse some more. If you play soccer, and you abhor kicking with your left foot, do it anyway. If you play basketball, and you just can't dribble with the opposite hand, keep trying.

The bottom line is that if you hate something in your sport, it can quickly turn into a fear. So, if you are telling yourself, you hate your driver, then you develop a fear of hitting drives. If you despise your 30-yard pitch shots, you will fear those. No fear! Love your driver now. Hating an aspect of your sport only derails your performance. Stretch yourself to embrace those areas you dread—right now! Reaching—exploring your full potential—equals winning performances in the future.

Mental Toughness Training Tip:

Figuring out a way to get comfortable when you are in an uncomfortable situation is extremely important. If you resist and try to avoid the uncomfortable, your progress will remain limited.

It took me a while to figure out that players will often avoid the shots that make them uncomfortable because they don't want to look bad in front of others or hinder their confidence.

We might all agree that bunker practice tends to be one of those universally disliked areas to practice in golf. One player told me that she felt really comfortable after practicing a few shots out of a bunker and quickly went on to practice on other strokes. When it came time to compete in a big tournament, she struggled hitting the first shot out, then the second, and then barely eked the third one out of the trap. She'd worked hard on other aspects of her game but failed to score because of those errors in the bunker—she hadn't prepared for that shot and rehearsed it for the "show."

In that moment, I realized that she had not made that weakness in her game a priority, so she was simply not ready when the pressure was on. Sure—as her coach, I should have been on it, but she even had me fooled because she acted so confident and prepared. She confessed later that she had a fear of bunkers and tried to avoid them—at all costs.

No matter what, uncomfortable situations arise on the course in pressure-filled moments. Be ready. Rehearse. Practice the shot. Reach. Always.

Mental Toughness Training Tip:

Work on your weaknesses and find ways to hone those areas. If you avoid certain areas of your game, undoubtedly, you will face them in competition. Own them! The true magic lies outside your comfort zone.

Another lesson in *reaching* happened before our first invitation to Nationals. I had recruited a super athlete and former basketball player who was very motivated but had a hard time making the top five golf team line-up, playing in the sixth position. Between spring and the next fall season, she went from sixth position to not only making the top line-up but becoming one of the top players on the team. Why? Her work ethic and commitment to the rehearsal in the off-season were focused and consistent.

She worked at a golf shop and after work without fail would practice putting for about 30 minutes. And I mean, religiously. She was disciplined about these personal practices and focused on her shots—and confidence—like she was in a tournament. Some players think it's quantity of time that is important, but it's the quality time that is critical. You can spend hours on the practice tee and see little improvement if you don't set an intention and purpose beforehand.

She had spent that break growing outside of her comfort zone and turned a weakness into a strength. It's human nature to avoid our challenge areas but deep dive preparation—physically, emotionally, and mentally—catapults us to broader mastery.

If you stay comfortable, plan on the same old performance.

In 2010, when PGA tour professional Graeme McDowell won the US Open at Pebble Beach, a reporter asked him afterwards how he had become such a tough player. McDowell said his toughness was because he had learned "to feel comfortable in uncomfortable situations." When I heard him say those words, I wrote them down and have tried to follow those words ever since.

Special Nugget for When Girls Win!

When Girls Win, we move outside our Comfort Zone to explore our potential and achieve more. We rehearse for any number of unforeseen scenarios.

Finding that Magic Zone is critical to our success. Period. In any walk of life. Sure, that means more challenges and failures will inevitably occur–that's all part of the fun!

TELL ME SOMETHING GOOD

Make sure your worst enemy doesn't live between your ears.

–Alex Morgan Olympic Gold Medalist, US women's soccer

A lesson that took me forever to learn as a player and that has truly helped me as a coach is perfecting that *voice* both inside and outside your head. We all have an inner dialogue running, or more often than not, an inner critic. We need to be aware of what we are thinking to ourselves as well as what we are saying out loud. Focusing the mind on what you are doing well is the fastest way to better performance.

Once while recruiting at a junior tournament, I overheard several high school players who had finished their rounds discussing their worst shots of the day. Not one of them mentioned anything good about their performance that day. Finally, I turned and asked the group if they'd had any good shots. Silence. Then one girl perked up and said, "Oh yeah, I just missed having a hole in one on number 14!" She smiled as everyone said things like, "Wow—that's so cool. Way to go!"

For a few moments, I felt like a proud coach who had just helped guide a young player to a more positive place. But in a matter of minutes, the talk quickly shifted back into low gear. The group started beating themselves up again with their negative words. The negative talk almost seemed like it was a contagious disease, and they all were suffering from it.

I felt sad as I kept thinking how I had done the same thing when I was their age. Yet, with all the recent research on the benefits of a positive mental attitude, the mental training books on the market, and quotable psychology gurus out there, I could not understand why this was still happening. I realize that a lot of it has to do with the social aspect of the game and talking about the negative shots after a round can easily become a habit developed at a young age.

For example, a parent might pressure a player after a round asking, "What happened on the 8th hole when you went out of bounds? Instead of saying, "Wow—that was an awesome shot you hit on 14?" See the difference? The emphasis on the negative will just keep spiraling out of control unless you observe it, realize it's become a detriment, and change the pattern. I wanted to help these young golfers get out of their own way, but I knew that was not a task I could tackle in few minutes.

The kids were peppering all this negative emotion into their subconscious minds without knowing it. Sports psychologist Dr. Bob Rotella says that people complain a lot about their putting for example, to be self-deprecating and socially cool. It's a habit and as humans we are wired with a negative bias—we have a tendency to beat ourselves up rather than pat ourselves on the back.[1] Then it becomes self-fulfilling sabotage as negative words hinder future performances.

I have had players say things like, "I had a great round today, but my putting sucked. I needed a calculator to total them up." Or, "I hate this course—I never play well on it." Or even, "I never can win; I always seem to finish in second or third." Additionally, I've had parents say things to me in front of their kids: "My daughter is a good player, but she's not good around the greens." Or "My daughter could be really good, but she makes too many poor course management decisions." Think of the emotion tied to these pessimistic and belittling statements. Will they help anyone perform better? No, they will not. The daughter is hearing these negative words and it's echoing in their subconscious brain, which will lead to derailing her play, especially in a clutch situation.

When I was in high school and started competing more, one of my negative habits was tracking my three-putts. A pro had told me that if I tracked my putting, I could analyze my round afterwards. He suspected that putting was keeping me from shooting lower scores. I would always add up my three-putts at the end and then say things like, "I shot a 77 but I three-putted six times, so if I hadn't done that, it would have been a 71." This way of thinking was a crazy way to make myself feel better since I had not measured up to my expectations. If I could blame one aspect of my game for my higher-than-expected score, I'd be able to escape responsibility for my performance.

A family member unintentionally added to my negative thinking about my putting as well. At a few junior tournaments that we both played in, he would say things to friends in front of me like, "Yeah, my sister can hit the ball, but she can't putt." I would just shake my head in agreement to confirm his words and further infuse that negative thought into my subconscious.

I didn't know this at the time, but my negative thoughts on my poor putting were compounding in my subconscious mind. I constantly confirmed to myself that I was a bad putter almost like I had an incurable illness. I spent hours working on my putting on the practice green. Just when I thought I had conquered it, I would enter a tournament, feel the pressure, miss a putt, doubt myself and then off on the downward spiral of despair I would go.

My subconscious mind had come to expect poor putting. I had engrained that negative notion so deeply into my brain that my subconscious mind was saying, "Three-putts are your thing MJ—let's go for more."

Mental Toughness Training Tip:

The key to more positive outcomes lies in your self-talk AND the stories you are telling yourself!! The more positive your thoughts, the more self-belief will inhabit your subconscious mind.

ACCENTUATE THE POSITIVE

So, what about this negative bias? Science proves that as humans we are wired to the negative bias. Our subconscious remembers—and focuses on—the negative stories and emotions more than the positive ones. We are built this way to help protect us against danger in the future. For example, when you are first learning to drive a car, your conscious mind is at work on where to put your hands on the steering wheel, how to look through your rearview mirror, and so on. Slowly, the subconscious starts taking over and performs without all that thinking. Say you are driving along and all of a sudden you see something in the middle of the road, and you innately swerve in order to miss it. Your subconscious reacted intuitively to the potential danger without losing precious time overthinking the situation.

In sports, the subconscious learns to take over to help you physically perform without any hesitation. As noted earlier, neuroscientists say that the subconscious mind controls about 95 percent of what we do as it handles everything our bodies need to function properly from eating to breathing. Training the subconscious mind is clearly the key to becoming mentally tougher.[2]

Here is the great news. The subconscious can be trained just as the body is strength-trained with weights, cardio exercises, yoga, and more. You can indeed train your subconscious mind to be more positive. And more good news: You can start this training right now!

One way to nurture your subconscious mind is affirmation training. In affirmation training, you tie a strong positive emotion to your words to help fortify your subconscious. Let's say you want to improve your putting, so you write an affirmation to yourself, "Your putting is improving, and you are a gifted putter." If in the back of your mind you are still saying, "Well that's a joke, you really suck at putting," then you've defeated the mission. You need to really feel your affirmation, believe it, breath into it, and then of course rehearse the physical aspect of the skill as well. Experts agree that affirmations are more effective in third person. Saying *"You* are a great putter" is better than *"I* am a great putter."

Mental Toughness Training Tip:

Writing positive affirmations and/or journaling about your successes and intentions will help invigorate your brain just like lifting weights strengthens your body.

You see, the subconscious is super powerful! What we dwell on, we will get more of. So, if you are saying, "I can never hit a fairway with my driver?" Guess what? More drives missing the fairway are in your future!

I talked to a former PGA tour pro with a consulting/teaching business not far from our college. He said his phone was ringing off the hook with desperate parents looking for the quick secret to improving before their child entered the next tournament. He said often parents are so desperate for their kid to become the next Tiger or Rory, Lexi, or Nelly, they'll pay whatever it takes to help them get there.

We all want that one magic bullet or physical tip that is going to redeem us and improve our performance. Problem is, it's not just about the mechanics of the sport—it's a positive and confident mindset that's the game changer. Obviously, better self-talk is not going to turn a 240-yard drive into a 300-yard drive, but it will infuse your game with the tenacity and determination to realize your higher potential when you play.

ENCOURAGING CHATTER ONLY, PLEASE!

We are constantly talking to ourselves. In fact, psychologist Rodney Korba's research indicates that our internal dialogue has an equivalent rate of speech in excess of 4,000 words per minute, which is 10 times that of verbal speech.[3] That's a lot of words! So, it's the inner chatter as well as the words we say out loud that are influencing how we behave and perform.

We had a player who was super fun and entertaining, but I didn't realize that she also used sarcasm to ease her anxiety. I didn't initially catch on to what she was really doing as she also made everyone around her laugh. I came to realize that even though she was super funny about her game and had us all in stiches, ultimately, her humor about her bad shots became detrimental to her performance.

Ridiculing yourself and broadcasting negative stories and beliefs out loud have an even greater impact on your performance than the thoughts you say quietly to yourself. One more time: saying invalidating and pessimistic stories out loud have an even greater negative impact on your performance than what you mutter under your breath.

Once this star player realized the impact of what she had been joking about out loud regarding her chipping, she was able to manage the negative voice and welcome the positivity required to achieve so much more—including winning a tournament with top competition and leading the team to a podium finish at Nationals!

WHY IS THE SPOKEN WORD SO POWERFUL?

According to sports psychologist and author of *It Takes What it Takes*, Trevor Moawad, saying something out loud, makes it ten times more powerful than if it's just a thought. Negativity is four to seven times more powerful than positivity.[4]

There are other studies that show that stating negative words out loud release negative hormones and neurotransmitters in the brain. While positive words stimulate the brain's frontal lobes, negative words trigger increased activity in the amygdala, which is the fear center of the brain.

Now look at the havoc you wreak on your game if you are speaking negative things out loud. You increase their influence and power over performance by 40-70 percent.

An example that Treavor Moawad gave on the Ed Mylett podcast[4] is a well-known story about Red Sox baseball player, Bill Buckner, and the ground ball that zipped through his legs in the 1986 World Series. Buckner had just said on the radio 20 days prior to the game that he didn't want to be the guy to let someone score with the ball going through his legs! Then it happened just as Buckner had feared. The Mets scored and won the World Series. Ouch!

A more recent example happened at the 2022 Winter Olympics. I admire US ski racer, Mikaela Shiffrin, and my heart hurt for her that she didn't accomplish what she set out to do. Instead of coming home with several gold medals, she fell in three straight events.

I am not sure what Mikaela's mindset was in the first two races, but in the third one, the Women's Super-Combined event, she seemed to be in perfect position to win a Gold Medal after the downhill portion. The event couples a downhill race and a slalom race, and the scores are combined to produce the winner. After the downhill, Mikaela, whose specialty is slalom, was in 5th place. She was the best slalom skier in the top 10 grouping, so if she stayed true-to-form, the gold medal was hers—and the announcers were really hyping that up.

Shortly before the slalom portion of the race, an ABC reporter interviewed her about how she was feeling. She admitted "I am NOT feeling totally confident with the slalom. I have a recurring image of me like skiing out on Gate 15 again. I am just going to try my best." And then she added, "I am not placing any bets, but yeah, I mean, at least I have a chance and that's great." Yikes.

I turned to my husband and said, "Oh no, I don't think she will get it done now. She said those words out loud about not feeling totally confident and not placing any bets on her." Remember Treavor Moawad's comments on the multiplier effect when you say something out loud? Mikaela's self-doubt spoken shortly before the race increased the probability of what she did *not* want to happen by 40-70 percent. We create a self-fulfilling prophesy when we profess our limitations and lack of confidence—*out loud!*

Mikaela got off to what looked like a great solid start and then it happened again. About 10 gates into the run, she lost her balance and fell. I clearly don't know the full story of her mindset or what she was going through that day, but I do know her words prior to the race may have had an impact on her subconscious mind and then became a self-fulfilling outcome.

WORK TO DO

So, what's the answer and how do you perform at your highest potential every time? Listen to the words you are saying. Watch both what you are telling yourself and what you are saying out loud. With awareness and positive self-talk, you can build a champion mindset.

If you are thinking, "That's it. That's all I need to do? You built a successful program from scratch by teaching your players to talk to themselves and their teammates more positively?" I would have to say, "Yes. That's played an enormous part in our success!" Of course, there is more to it than voice, but it starts with the words you are saying—personally and as a team. They matter. *Big Time.*

Golf is one sport that truly parallels life. For example, if you spill your coffee in the morning and start your day in a frustrated mood, that negative thought can lead to other negative thoughts and the day quickly becomes a bad day. Same thing happens in golf. You hit a less than desirable shot, negative words pop in, fear arises, and if the negativity and self-doubt creep in, you will not play to your potential that day.

Even now after all the mind-over-matter research and scientific proof of the power of negative mindset and talk, I still hear players say things like, "I guess I don't have it today" even after only playing two or three holes. How can you "not have it today" only after a few holes? You gave up on yourself. Your inner voice just told you to *give up!* Maybe you didn't physically walk off the course conceding, but you abandoned yourself and your game. Your mind called it quits. I've trained our players to work hard on speaking positively to themselves and it works. It's a process, just like any type of training, but eventually it really pays off.

It's interesting how many negative things I hear as I'm recruiting new players with high potential. I hear about the bad holes that wrecked the score. I hear about how the weather was miserable, or the green speeds were too fast, so they couldn't sink the putts. Would you go to a job interview and tell the employer why you didn't perform so well at your last job? Hopefully, not. But it's amazing how many recruits focus on excuses for their scores or what is not working with their games.

If you are only focusing on what is going wrong and making excuses, how do you expect to improve in that area? I've heard players say "Yes, I have learned how to score, but I know I could shoot lower if I didn't three-putt so much." Or, "My game is great from tee to green for the most part, only my chipping is awful." And I always smile at this one: "My stroke average is around 76, but I usually have a few blow-up holes, so without them, I would be easily around 73 or 74 each round!"

Please! Let go of all the negative!

Mental Toughness Training Tip:

The voice in your head can either help you win or help you lose. You get to choose. Focus on a positive voice and talk to yourself like you would talk to a teammate or friend. Be affirmative and anticipate positive outcomes.

WHAT'S YOUR MANTRA?

After researching and understanding mental toughness training more, I had an insightful discussion with a LPGA player who had worked directly with Dr. Bob Rotella and was in Portland for the LPGA Portland Classic. She shared a list of words and phrases he had given her to explore what clicked with her when she was playing. She could say those things to herself and replace the negative voices with the positive phrases that resonated with her. Phrases like:

- Waste no energy on uncontrollable outside factors.
- Focus on what you CAN control not outside factors.
- Make your mind and your emotions your edge.
- Place a low level of importance on each shot.
- Positive vibes only; there's no place for worry.

I then had our players find phrases on the list that resonated with them. They wrote them down on cards and put them on their push carts during the next tournament. One player was committed to two of the phrases and every time I saw her for the final round, she smiled and said to me, 'Worry is wasteful" and "Success does not mean perfection." She just kept smiling and seemed so peaceful and free every time I saw her on the course. She was feeding those words to herself all day long and then, BAM! She shot a personal best that day—her first under-par round!

Author and motivational speaker Jon Gordon says, "learn to talk to yourself instead of listen to yourself,"[5] and that is exactly what our player did. When the negative voice tried to override which happened as she got closer to finishing, she was able to silence it quickly. Her kinder voice piped up: "worry is wasteful" and "be indifferent to mistakes" and she moved on.

I will never forget that magical day for her as I witnessed the power of her affirmative self-talk and felt her confident energy. After the round, she told me she'd always wanted to believe that it was a physical or technical component of her swing was holding her back not her negative voice. This time, she was aware of the power of the voice and found success. As a longtime coach, I've learned that self-sabotage due to negative self-talk is rampant. We all do it. Even the better players—and coaches—are at its mercy.

Mental Toughness Training Tip:

Be your loudest cheerleader. Realize it's the negative self-talk that creates tension, stress, and defeat. Commit to positivity and confident self-talk and you will see an immediate difference in your performance.

As for my putting story? As I learned more about the subconscious mind from various psychologists, I realized that I had just trained my subconscious mind to believe that I was a bad putter and that became my identity. I was great on the practice green, but then when my game was under pressure or I was in a clutch situation, I would miss. I let self-doubt arise—unwelcomed. And unfortunately, it stayed. Once I really learned the power of my voice, I was able to train my subconscious, and that's when I realized I was actually a great putter.

Special Nugget for When Girls Win!

When Girls Win, we stop beating ourselves up with our words. Negative thoughts will still arise, but our mental strength will help us respond more effectively and positively.

We are kinder to ourselves and speak to ourselves and to others with much more grace and empathy. We have self-compassion and are gentler on ourselves for mistakes we make. Most importantly we forgive ourselves and choose a higher vibration like gratitude, joy, and love to progress. We know that mistakes will occur and they are there to help us learn and improve.

12

EYE OF THE STORM

If you want to play, you have to play with boys.
If you want to stick around, you have to beat them.

–Annika Sorenstam, LPGA Hall of Fame

We had some unusually grisly weather at one spring conference championship event held in Washington, off the Puget Sound. The rain was blasting sideways with wind gusts up to 35 mph and the windchill factor was in the 30's. The conditions were nearly unplayable on Day One of the two-day event, and by Day Two, conditions deteriorated even more with thunderstorms rolling in.

Our players were pulled off the course after just a few holes due to lightning strikes closing in on the area. All the men's and women's teams competing huddled inside the clubhouse waiting in soggy rain gear to see if the weather would improve or if the final round would be canceled. If so, the scores of Day One would stand as the final results.

SOMETIMES YOU GOTTA MAN UP

I decided to check in to see what the golf professionals were seeing on the radar screen in the pro shop and what the vibe was regarding continuing play or not. As I walked over that way, I overheard another coach down the hall speaking to a few other coaches say, "We just need to man up." It made me laugh out loud as I immediately knew where he stood on continuing the play.

I am truly fine with manning up if that's what I need to do. However, continuing a competition when it no longer resembles golf is a different story. If umbrellas are turning inside out, greens start pooling with small lakes, and players are draped in so much constrictive clothing they look like they belong on a ski slope, then perhaps we need to reconsider.

DO THE RIGHT THING

The wait continued for all of us as the golf professionals were trying to determine the distance of the lightning strikes and if the course would still be playable. As the storm raged on, it became evident that ending the tournament was the best thing to do for our players. The temperature was still dropping, everyone was drenched, and we'd waited long enough in our wet gear. Given all the factors, I was in favor of cancelling the second round.

No matter if it is weather or other conditions or situations, as coaches, we are responsible for the well-being of our players—regardless of where you stand on the leaderboard. Our team was in first after Day One, but that was not why I was in favor of canceling. I also had a player who had a chance to win National Player of the Year, and she was not in the lead. This could hurt her chances if we didn't get to play it out so she could perhaps win the tournament. At the same time, we needed to look at what was best for the entire group.

I wish it was as simple as speaking up and pointing out the obvious based on the facts, but unfortunately, at this point in my career, I had learned that many decisions are not made that way. They are made prior to the meetings in private discussions, so the best chance of getting your point across and your fact-based opinion heard had to happen outside the meeting room first.

I knew the vote to cancel was close, so now it was time to get creative and make a move. I had a couple of aces in my pocket because I knew most of the players did not want to go back out. They were done and the coaches knew they were done. My idea was to find allies—not unlike the television show, *Survivor*—and figure out how to make it happen.

Mental Toughness Training Tip:

Figure out ways to get to yes by being tactical and smart. Understand all the facts and be willing to make the case that's best for all even if the loudest voices believe differently.

TAKE A VOTE

It did not take long to realize where everyone stood and the coach who just might be the deciding vote. He was a new coach and his men's team was in second place, but his women's team clearly did not want to go back out. I caught up with him near the clubhouse exit and asked him to go outside with me to chat for a minute. Just as we opened the door, we got a blast of icy rain in our faces, so we stayed just inside the door to converse. I could tell he agreed about the unplayable conditions, so I just added a few thoughts. I told him that one of the quickest ways to earn respect from your players is to make sure they know that you are putting them first.

We went back in toward the main room, but I wasn't certain which way he would decide. It was time for the coaches to huddle to make the decision. No discussion ensued—we just went straight to the vote.

The coaches all voted to keep playing just as I had predicted, but the new coach voted for cancelling. His one vote brought us to the majority. I was so relieved that I jumped out of my chair—not because that meant we'd win the tournament, rather that it was truly the right thing to do for our players!

Within seconds, the entire room where the players were located erupted with happy screams and high fives. The majority were relieved, not wanting to continue. Teams quickly grabbed their things and headed for their vans to hit the road and drive home.

A few days after the tournament, I learned that the one of the coaches filed a complaint with the conference. Apparently, he said the vote had been manipulated so our team could pick up an automatic win. Huh? Didn't we collectively vote on cancelling the tourney given all the brutal conditions? Surprises happen both on and off the golf course.

Later that year, a new bylaw was added to our procedure manual that stated only the golf professional at a conference championship event, our Conference Commissioner and the rules officials can make a cancellation call in the future. The coaches were no longer allowed to be involved.

> *Mental Toughness Training Tip:*
>
> *Do what you believe is right! You are not always going to win, but always stand up for what you think is right. Fortitude is powerful.*

GO THE DISTANCE

A few years later, at another conference championship event, our new rule was tested when a severe storm was predicted to sweep in about 1 p.m.—and everyone knew it. The rules officials knew it. The conference knew it. The host coaches knew it. We all knew it.

Our team was the second to last group to tee off at 11 a.m., so we knew for certain that our team would get hit with the worst of it on the back nine. This happened during the Covid period where teams played together with their own teammates in fivesomes. We were also paired by school with men's teams playing between the women's team, so the nearest women's team finished a full two holes ahead of us. We were for sure going to get caught in the worst of the storm.

After we finished 9 holes, the forecasters were right as the storm hit and the temperature dramatically dropped. The wind picked up and the rain started pelting us sideways. I asked the host coach if the rules officials would be out monitoring the conditions, to which she told me yes, the tournament committee would be checking.

There was a rules official that drove by a few times, but we never saw a committee member or course professional—not that I blame them. On one hole, we broke three large golf umbrellas in the strong wind gusts. Even if the umbrellas had remained intact, the playing conditions were ruthless. By the luck of the draw, some teams had finished up before the storm even hit and we still had at least two more hours to battle the elements—trying to play in something that definitely no longer resembled a sport.

The rules official sympathized with us but said there was not enough pooling of water on the greens for him to stop play. That was up to a committee. There is no way a professional golfer would have been playing in the conditions we were faced with—especially with the freezing temperatures and the struggle to even hold onto a club. Were we being punished?

WIN THE DAY

But guess what? We persevered and we won that day—both in terms of the tournament but more importantly in understanding an inner strength within each of us that we didn't even know existed. I had never witnessed such a strong mentally tough team. They continued to cheer each other on and ignored the adversity that literally kept battering them. Their will and positive spirit was truly inspirational!

With relentless determination we finished in the dark. When I left the scoring area with my players, including one who had just won medalist for the first time in a Conference Championship event, there was no ceremony or awards. Despite being visibly shaking from the cold, we celebrated our grit with soaking wet hugs, sprinted for the van and turned the heater on blast mode.

This time, I knew we no longer needed to peel out of the parking lot to show anyone anything. We had won our inner games that day and stayed in it as a team with unshakeable spirit and love, and in the end, that is all that mattered. We manned up—even though we shouldn't have been asked to.

Like the moral of *When the Grinch Stole Christmas*, we learned that no matter what, no one can take away your heart or spirit.

How does this apply to you as a player? Nothing comes easy. You must be mentally prepared at any time for any situation, particularly the surprises.

Mental Toughness Training Tip:

Create that steel bubble around you and fill it with mantras that keep you in a super confident, powerful place and enjoy the challenge. The strength you gain during adversity is unsurpassable.

Special Nugget for When Girls Win!

When Girls Win, we are more courageous, dauntless, and gutsy than we are given credit for. We know we are meant for greatness—and we press on. We never let anyone rain on our parade!

YOU GET WHAT YOU GIVE

Take those chances and you can achieve greatness,
whereas if you go conservative, you'll never know.

–Danica Patrick, former Indy car racer

P*rocess* is a key sports word bantered about these days. "Follow your process; It's all a process; remember to stick with your process; the process will get you there." Understanding exactly what the process is and how to embrace it can be very confusing.

Process is the commitment and discipline it takes on your journey to reach your goals. It's the daily work it takes to stay consistent and keep growing. Sometimes athletes have to take a step backwards, readjust and learn new tactics in order to move forward—which is all part of the process. When someone doesn't quite achieve what they want, they are usually told by their parents or coach, "Remember, it's a process." It is ongoing work to get to that end goal. As many of us have heard: "Don't be discouraged; it's a process."

Dr. Bob Rotella says, "Process goals are the to-do lists of striving for excellence. That process is what gives you a chance to find out how good you can be."[1] Instead of focusing on results, set actual process goals for a round of golf to see how well you can play.

I was at a tournament several years ago in the Bay Area where one of our players exclaimed in a frustrated tone, "I am staying with my process Coach, but I keep making bogeys and my score is just going higher. My process is not working." I told her to stay with her process. At the same time, though, I thought, *I need to do a much better job of explaining how process goals work as there was no doubt that she was too focused on the results and not the process.*

BE THE BALL

A process goal for golf might be something like, "I will visualize and commit to my target on every shot." If my player had that process goal and had visualized and committed to her target on every shot, then she would be doing her process. The key is to *only* judge yourself on sticking with your process—not on results. Judging on results takes you away from what you can control whereas process is about doing something that you can control.

A mind that is too results-oriented derails being the best you can be in that moment. Sadly, our player was focusing on her score rather than visualizing and committing to her target.

When Rory McIlroy won the Open Championship in 2014 at Royal Liverpool, the broadcast caught his caddie reminding Rory on one of the last fairways of the final round, "Stay with your process." I jumped out of my chair! Yes! This works!

Rotella was validated and the process was right on. I read several stories after Rory's victory and found that he had two process goals. "With my long shots, I just wanted to stick to my process and stick to making good decisions, making good swings."[2] He wasn't very specific if that meant visualizing his shot or committing to his target, but he clearly had a process on every shot and stayed with it.

"And for my putting, I was just picking a spot on the green and then trying to roll it over my spot every time. I wasn't thinking about holing it. I wasn't thinking about what it would mean or how many further ahead it would get me. I just wanted to roll that ball over that spot."[2]

There was no needless chatter going on like, "Hey, you might win this today," or "You are 3 under now and if you can birdie the last two holes, you'll be good to go." It was all about the process and surrendering the outcome.

Mental Toughness Training Tip:

Focus on your daily process goals and the results will take care of themselves.

NEVER GIVE UP ON A GOOD THING

Early on in my coaching career, I had a lot of players who focused heavily on what they were shooting saying. "I'm 1 over after 9 and going on to shoot my best score ever!" Right then, I knew it wasn't going to happen. Once your mind moves to an *outcome orientation*, you are not playing in the moment but trying to control something that you simply can't. You are limiting your ability to perform at your highest level by focusing on score or outcome.

I have won some local club tournaments, but it took me awhile to understand how to let go of counting up my score (outcome oriented) and to just stay with my process goal. I seemed to stay with my process until I had a few bogeys, and then I thought if I focused more on what I was shooting, I could *control* it a little more and make some birdies happen. Wrong! That is not how it works.

Once, I had one of my best under par rounds on the front 9 in the final round of a tournament and knew I was quite possibly in the lead heading into the back 9. I was so proud of myself for the competitive score that I abandoned my process and started thinking about how cool it was going to be to win that day! I was already standing on the podium, thinking about how excited my husband was going to be and celebrating my victory. And all that with 9 holes still left to play!

It's easy to get swept away when you feel the magic and you're in that flow state. You don't think it will fade away. I was wrong on that one. I proceeded to double bogey the 10th hole and triple the 11th. And just like that, my great momentum majorly shifted. I ended up losing the tournament by one stroke. I had bailed on process and thought somehow, I could control the outcome.

If you focus too hard on score, you simply aren't in the flow. You're left controlling brain is pushing you, and it's difficult to get into your zone. Lighten up and immerse in a carefree place where it's almost like you don't care. How can I get to that state when I do care? Of course, we care, but we have to be willing to *detach from the outcome* and focus on the stroke-by-stroke process to achieve our best play.

Many people assume that elite athletes are born with mental and emotional toughness genes and that's why they are so successful. While they may have been blessed with the physical prowess to help them in their sport, they were *not* born mentally tough. Mental and emotional toughness is learned. If you skip the training, the process, or doubt the importance of it, you will find yourself struggling in those clutch situations. Most importantly, you will limit your full potential and greatness.

Mental Toughness Training Tip:

You can't control results, but you CAN control your process. Remember to celebrate the little victories as you pursue the bigger picture. Learn how to be process-oriented, and you will become much stronger in your sport.

Special Nugget for When Girls Win!

When Girls Win, while we are striving for incredible results, we need to be in the moment. When our mind says, "think ahead about the score and how you want to finish," we lose the power of the moment and our process. Show up, do the work, and trust your process. Really. It's the only way to shine and achieve the results you want!

14

UNDER PRESSURE

Pressure is a privilege.

–Billie Jean King, U.S. Tennis Hall of Fame

It was our fourth consecutive visit to the NCAA National Championship, and we had just finished the normal prep process in the van. The energy was high. We are more experienced now with how we prepare for success, including spinning the right tunes to get us in a winning mindset—a critically important key to a great performance as we've learned!

This particular year the National Championship is taking place in Destin, Florida, in the panhandle. The first match of the four-round 72-hole Championship starts today. Our team has prepared for The Show—the Big Stage—all season long and we can't wait to tee it up.

We pull into the parking lot and see a row of our competitors' vans. I take a deep breath but feel so calm this time. As the players are hopping out of the van *I Gotta Good Feeling* by Flo Rida is blasting from our speakers and the warm beach air feels welcoming.

Our players are unloading their gear while I am at the front passenger side door standing on the running board struggling to free our team duffel bag which is wedged between the two front seats. Without any warning, I hear a soft voice whisper behind me "Please make the pressure go away."

"Wait, what?!" I say to myself as I almost hit my head on the ceiling of the van. I turn my head around to see one of our top players standing there with a look of complete fear on her face. I can't speak for a minute—which is unlike me—so I whip my head around and give another tug on the duffel to stall for time. My mind is whirling with what I can possibly say. Did I just hear her correctly?

I take a deep breath and nonchalantly say over my shoulder "It's okay, you'll be fine," and then I calmly followed it up with "You know you know what to do out there, just do it." I slowly turn around now with the duffel in my hand to find the player hasn't budged. She is standing frozen like a statue; eyes glazed over and seems desperate for a better answer. For a split second, I think maybe we'd emphasized *chill* too much for our process goal that day. I rely on that inner humor to help me navigate my own panic starting to bubble up.

"Please, Coach, make this feeling go away," she says again in a whisper. As an empath, I start to feel her enormous fear myself. It's palpable. I stare out toward the course still searching for a helpful response. This was clearly not part of our visualization and relaxation script we had just played in the van.

I motion her to come back into the van and sit down with me for a minute as she is the last teammate to tee off that day. The other players are ready to go, standing around waiting—I can tell they are becoming concerned about their teammate. I urge them to start warming up and let them know we're just going to listen to a little more music to get us in the groove. I choose some spa tunes to create a calming vibe.

PRESSURE IS OUR FRIEND; FEAR IS A LIAR

This dilemma taught me just how fear has a sneaky way of haunting an athlete at any moment and in any situation. I did not see or antici- pate this coming at all, nor did I ever suspect it would capture one of our best players who had been in her zone and playing great golf all season long. Even though we had been preparing hard for this moment, out of nowhere, fear reared its head, grabbed her, and pulled her deep into panic mode—all just an hour and a half before she needed to compete.

I knew this player was feeling the pressure as one of the best D-III players in the nation—and we both knew that she had a chance to win a national honor award. Now, without warning, she is questioning if she has a game, a process or even a swing for that matter.

I am reminded of my own nerves and anxiety at our first National Championship when I threw my game plan out the window and chased after the other coaches on the first day to see what they were doing. I didn't trust myself in that big moment. I decide to tell her that story about my own sense of panic to see if I can make her laugh and relax. She cracks a slight smile, but I know she needs more.

I have to dig deep now. I tell her that she is being lied to by fear and remind her of the acronym often used to describe fear: False Evidence Appearing Real. She gives me a sheepish nod but says nothing.

As a reminder, the natural response when we sense fear is the fight or flight response. The body wants to run in order to escape those distressing feelings. Unfortunately, if you run or try to push it away, the pressure or fear will grow stronger and become even more debilitating.

Fear from pressure feels so real, intense, and scary but if you acknowl- edge it's just an apparition, a lie, you can reverse it. In fact, in Todd Hermann's book, *The Alter Ego Effect*, he says, "It's a good idea to name your fear, personify it, so when it does hit, you can laugh at it, cajole it, and move on......You can give it a name. Make the enemy as small as possible. Make it cute. Take away all its fear over you. Make it the most non-threatening thing, like a puppy and call it Scooby-Doo."[1]

Mental Toughness Training Tip:

Pressure is your friend and fear is a liar. When pressure arrives, observe it, embrace it, honor it and you will break its stronghold. When you break through the resistance, you're on your way to the next level!

AIN'T NO STOPPIN' US NOW

We're still sitting in the van. I ask my player about her family and her boyfriend to engage her, and she relaxes a bit more. I remind her that she is not defined by her golf game and most importantly, her score. It's strange how we all know this as athletes, but when pressure—and fear—arise, our first thought is to run from it. We may succumb to it and crazy notions like our family won't love us anymore if we don't perform well. I don't completely get it, as even with a strong self-identity, it happens. I must admit, I've done it. I've caved into fear.

In the end, it is our ego that is barraged by fear—the ego is afraid of failing and looking bad. After a lot of research and reading, I have learned that the ego likes to control things and is responsible for our self-criticism. Unfortunately, when pressure mounts, our ego likes to dominate even more and pushes additional fear in. Instead of trusting everything we've learned and mastered, we get stuck believing the lies that fear is telling us.

The anticipation of the moment is where pressure exists. It's the prime time when our imagination inspires false stories and becomes more intense. I knew the player would be fine once she got on the course—we all know the anticipation of that first shot is the hardest. It can feel like waiting for an operation—or the results of an exam. The preoccupation might drag our mind into the *what-if game* and then the downward spiral into the endless rabbit hole of negativity begins.

Most competitors feel butterflies before a performance. If that anxiety takes a toll on you, the goal is to just change its meaning in your mind. Instead of thinking, *Oh no, this is scary,* you should think instead, *Oh, this means something important is about to happen.* It's all in how you perceive and approach that fear and anxiety. If you can approach it with the feelings that it's only going to help you, you will be that much better prepared for it. Someone once said, "make sure your butterflies are all going in the same direction" which is a great visual.

Mental Toughness Training Tip:

Trust all your hard work and your preparation. Let go of the false stories.

I'm still working with the anxious player when suddenly I remembered what Dr. David Cook said at our coach's convention. I told her the story he told about a player who had just earned his PGA card to compete on the PGA tour. He was in his 40's and beat out a bunch of younger, seemingly more talented guys. When the player was asked how he had accomplished that, he said, "I like to put myself in position where I feel like I'm choking my guts out, so I can see how good I can become. You see other people running from pressure. My whole purpose is to put my foot on the line each day and feel the heat because where I intend to go is a place of fire."[2]

When I said those words to the player, she looked at me kind of funny —almost like she was ready to choke her own guts out. "I guess this means I'm ready then," she said, finally breaking her silence.

This star athlete went on to have one of the best rounds of the day and then won the National Player of the Year award just two days later. She finished the Championship as National Runner-Up and was ranked #1 in the nation. I was thrilled that our mind-over-matter chat in the van had helped her mitigate the fear and use pressure in her favor.

Mental Toughness Training Tip:

Pressure can make you feel like you are going to choke your guts out, but that's why the best athletes embrace the discomfort and accept the situation. They know that in doing so, they can persevere and achieve so much more.

SOMETHING BIG

"I believe it's impossible to overestimate the importance of the mind in golf!" Dr. Bob Rotella emphasizes.

But many people get nervous talking about the mental aspect of the game. Even my husband tried to steer me away from saying "mental toughness training" thinking it may give the impression that I'm a psychologist, doctor or even a hypnotist. The fact is, I've just learned so much about how to manage one's mindset and attitude during competition, it's become a core component of my coaching.

I now know how critical the mind and mindset are to performance— especially in high-pressure, high-stakes situations. It's critical to focus as much on your mental game as your physical game. I have had many less experienced players score better than some highly ranked players due to their mental and emotional preparation for the pressure.

They put in the work way before the day of the competition with visualization training. Many athletes resist doing visualization but it's one of the most powerful things you can do. Most sports psychologists highly recommend even doing a script beforehand to help you be ready to stay composed during the most intense times.

Programming your mindset ahead of time is fundamental. I thought my star player was dialed into the zone and ready, but she succumbed to negative thoughts as pressure mounted and fear took over. Once she honored the pressure and thought about it differently, the tension eased in her body, and she was able to trust herself and her hard work.

One way to manage negative thoughts is to quickly change your body language. Stand taller. Walk with more swag. Visualize success. Tell your body it's ready. Bask in confidence. Own your game.

That rush of adrenaline we get when we sink the 20-footer, make a great play, score for your team to win just before the buzzer, hit a home run—any reward from a skilled performance—is why we play.

When everything is on the line, and you embrace the pressure to come out the other side as a champ, it's the best feeling in the world. Learning to thrive in that intensity gives us power and we're able to achieve so much more!

A FEW OF THE BEST THINGS YOU CAN DO:

1. Keep working on affirmations—write down how you are going to enjoy the competition. You have a choice to be excited and control what you can control—your mind!
2. Remember to breathe. Deep rhythmic breaths. Deep breathing exercises really reduce the cortisol levels of stress and allow more oxygen into your bloodstream so you can think more clearly.
3. Visualize yourself arriving at the competition in a positive space—or bubble—where negative thoughts or outside uncontrollable factors are never allowed inside. Visualize a protective shield around you throughout the competition!

Mental Toughness Training Tip:

Be aware of tension in your body, feel it, and do a body scan before you compete. Breathe into any tense areas, visualize healing light, and observe the tension leaving your body. Experiencing yourself letting go of that tension is one of the best things you can do before a performance.

Special Nugget for When Girls Win!

When Girls Win, as Billie Jean King says, "Pressure is a privilege." We make pressure and fear our friends. We embrace pressure and honor fear knowing they are preparing us to get to advance, excel. The pressure of competition is a gift enabling us to further channel our greatness.

15

LOVE YOURSELF

Say nice things to yourself because you're the only one listening.

–Gabrielle Bernstein, New York Times best-selling author, spiritual guru

S hortly after our first trip to the National Championship site, we traveled to the Santa Rosa Country Club in California to play in a Division-II tournament hosted by Sonoma State. It was an honor to be invited, as all the other teams were in a bigger division and had higher rankings than our team. The coach hosting the tournament knew of our strength as a D-III team at this point and sent us an invitation, which we gratefully accepted. I have always believed playing against tougher competition is the fastest way to improve. Rigorous competition requires you to dig deeper, and the lessons become much more valuable.

One of our players had just received a brand-new set of irons and asked me if she could use them in this tournament. My initial reaction was a firm no. I thought such a big change during competition may be too much and I didn't want her struggling during play and then blaming the new clubs for potential mistakes. She kept insisting that she was hitting her new irons better than her old ones, and finally wore me down. She promised me that the clubs would not be the problem and she took full responsibility for the decision.

During the first round, this player competed well against the field on a very tough track with tricky and large undulated greens. She posted a score near her average in the high 70s—all with her new clubs. The set-up for this tournament was extra-long at over 6,000 yards—by all means a challenging track. The greens were not only formidable but very quick with tough pin locations, so scores ran on average higher, with the lowest score of the day being a 72, just one under par. During the entire practice round and first day of the tournament, this player told me several times that she was loving her clubs and knew she was ready to score low with them. Her confidence was contagious, and I could feel her excitement and brilliant energy.

What I didn't realize was that she was going to do something really special the next day.

Meanwhile, another one of our top players also shot in the high 70s for the first round which was well above her average. I could sense she was feeling defeated and not living up to her expectations and those of her teammates. I encouraged her, pointing out that the course was playing more challenging for everyone, and reminded her that it was a two-day tournament, so this was only half-time. She practiced hard after the first round and seemed well-prepared for the second and final round.

The final round was a shotgun start where the entire field tees off on different holes at the exact same time. However, because of dense fog blanketing the course in the early morning hours, the start time kept getting pushed back due to challenging visibility issues.

The driving range and putting greens remained closed until about 10 minutes before play was to begin. None of the competitors from any teams had adequate time to warm-up and the host allowed each player just six range balls for practice. Of course, weather situations occur at golf events and are out of our control. Players must learn to adapt to these changes, or it can derail their mindset and negatively impact their attitude. Our team seemed to be in a good place handling the situation, and we were off!

Mental Toughness Training Tip:

Master your mindset and attitude. Reminder to release things you cannot control. The more you detach from all the things that are out of your control, the more you can focus on what you can guide—your mind and your attitude!

Our player with the new irons got off to a terrific start. She birdied a few holes early on and made the turn at two under par. When I stopped to check on her on the 9th hole, I could see a glazed-over look in her eyes—in a good way! I knew the look and could sense she was in that magical place we call *the zone* the moment I saw her. It's hard to explain the look exactly—and it's different for each player. But after coaching for so many years, I can see the fluidity and confidence and I know the look—she had it. I could tell she had confidently found her stride and was completely in the flow of her game.

I immediately knew that something special was happening and the best thing I could do was to stand back, observe, and just cheer her on as her iron shots landed like precision darts heading straight at the bullseye. As her coach, it gave me chills watching her perform. It's what you strive for as a coach—seeing your player in that incredible place where they are so thoroughly immersed in their game. Nothing is bothering them, and they are completely at ease. Their game is in-the-ultimate flow state, and they are just letting it happen. Being in this state didn't mean that every shot was going perfectly for her, but I knew she was at pure peace within herself, and no negativity or self-criticism existed. Yes, indeed, the zone is truly a magical place. I knew she was on a roll so left her to check on my other four players.

HOLD YOUR HEAD UP

I returned to watch another of our top players who earlier was struggling to find her own flow. I immediately knew she was still not in her usual confident place. She was fighting the game within the game—her mind. Her walk was slower and more hesitant than her normal stride and her slumped shoulders and body language told me that she was discouraged. Once I caught up to her, she looked at me with a blank look, and said in a low, monotone voice, "My game is just not here again today." She was more discouraged than ever. I left my cart to walk with her and witnessed her completely miss a green with her approach shot. I saw nothing but fear in her face.

Finally, I turned to her and said rather sternly, "I have an important question for you. Do you love yourself?" She looked at me kind of stunned and didn't say anything. I said, "Look, I love myself, so what about you? Do you love yourself?" In hearing that I loved myself she started laughing! I was happy that I at least was able to get her to crack a smile and laugh for a second—for just a few moments her fear disappeared.

I told her that I was reading a book about love and fear, and that if she was not choosing to love herself, fear would get the upper hand. We talked more about the powerful feeling of self-love as we walked toward her ball, and she became more self-aware when she realized that she had been ruthlessly criticizing herself and let the power of fear rule. She was seeing mistakes piling up and she had fallen into a deep negative rabbit hole.

How helpful is that when you are competing? Why would you let your last shot dictate what you are going to do with the next?

Just acknowledging the notion of self-love—and team-love—freed her to find better momentum with her game. Nothing technically changed with her physical swing, but she shifted her posture, started walking a little taller and found her confidence. Body language is extremely important to signal your mind that you are either feeling confident or not. As her posture changed, her attitude improved, and she regained her stride.

When she finally realized that it wasn't some technicality in her swing but her mind and attitude that were getting in her way, she was free to be herself. What she feared might happen—shooting a high score—was happening. The more she feared that she was going to shoot a high score, the more she created that reality and the less self-love and confidence she felt for herself.

Wash, rinse, repeat. It was a domino effect.

My job was to catch her from that freefall and get her mind back on track so she could have fun and enjoy her game. Happily, she rallied back with a strong finish, shooting one under on the last four difficult holes.

> *Mental Toughness Training Tip:*
>
> *CHANGING your negative body language is one of the fastest ways to adjust your pessimistic vibe and arrive in a more positive state or flow. Simply adjusting your posture, standing tall and walking with confidence signals your mind that you've located your inner power and are in rhythm. It works and is quickly effective.*

HIGHER LOVE

Self-love may sound deep or silly to some, but in the end, it is that compassion for yourself that is required to perform at your highest level. Self-love protects you from fear. Fear is unable to invade your mind if you are in a loving state—like our player with the new clubs!

The difference between the two players was not in their talent. It was not in their physical swings. It was not in their experience as players. It was not because they started on different holes or that one had a new set of clubs and the other did not. It was how they were walking and talking to themselves, and how they were evaluating themselves inwardly as they played. The difference in their performances was purely in how they were feeling about themselves: one was in a joyful place, completely immersed in the moment and free from thinking about the outcome, while the other player was beating herself up for not playing better and succumbing to fear of the outcome let alone what others might think of her.

One had found *the zone* and a Zen-like mode because she was accepting every shot no matter what. The other was shooting higher than normal because she was counting shots and becoming increasingly afraid of her final score and losing. She was falling into the trap that the score and results defined her as a person.

As a coach, I drive this home to my players: let go of the outcome and know that a score or a performance does not define who you are as a person. Befriending your kind inner voice is critical in challenging situations—especially if your coach isn't always there to tell you to love yourself!

Mental Toughness Training Tip:

Ask yourself, in the heat of battle, do you want an enemy speaking to you or an ally? Of course, you want an ally, a best friend saying nice things to you and cheering you on. Change the tone in your head, be kinder to yourself and embrace the magic.

Can you guess the outcome? My joyful player went on to shoot a personal best and record low round of 69—4 under par! She set a course record for that tournament on that course. She also tied the lowest round for a female at the country club playing from the longer yardage of the men's tees!

She knew she could do it and most importantly, she *believed* she could do it. She had no expectations or limits on what she was capable of doing. She completely found her zone, stepped on the gas pedal, and allowed it to happen.

The other player who was losing her mojo with frustration and trying too hard did end up rallying back on those last four holes and finished in a good spot. She also learned the importance of positive mental attitude and self-love—which was a huge takeaway and experience. Note: She then followed it up with a big win at the next tournament which was a conference championship event where she won medalist honors.

Self-awareness, especially in pressure situations is a key asset to becoming mentally stronger—and an elite athlete. Observing your fear, your mindset and then choosing love and positivity enable us to perform at higher levels.

Special Nugget for When Girls Win!

When Girls Win, we are less critical of ourselves. We stop comparing and judging. We live in the moment and for the moments. We are grateful and joyful. We exude confidence, positive body language and always walk with pep in our step, head held high.

True Confidence comes from loving yourself!

16

AIN'T NO MOUNTAIN HIGH ENOUGH

Courage, sacrifice, determination, commitment, toughness, heart, talent, guts. That's what little girls are made of; the heck with sugar and spice.

–Bethany Hamilton, Surfer

"Grit is passion and perseverance for long-term and meaningful goals." That's the definition developed by Angela Duckworth, Ph.D., the psychology professor, and researcher who coined the term *grit* in 2007. She determined that grit was a better predictor of success than IQ or talent.

I attribute a big part of our team's success over the years to grit. We are a smaller D-III school where most players focus on the importance of academics and their major first and foremost. Golf and playing on a competitive team are also important but we're not playing in the mighty D-I league, nor do our players have an opportunity to arrive with an athletic scholarship. What does that mean? We have more to prove and that's where grit comes in!

From the beginning of our program, our players and I have worked exceedingly hard to build a reputation of excellence—and grit. Each year our new recruits are driven to excel knowing that others before them have paved a solid path to award-winning distinction. Each incoming team honors the legacy of the past and continues to reach for more. They know our culture was created to ensure we keep climbing higher and make those alums, our supporters, fans, family members and community proud.

As a coach, I have found deep down the grit and perseverance I didn't even know I had. I wanted to keep evolving and growing our program and ensuring that necessary changes were in place to make us even better. I kept looking for ways to keep the team—and myself— progressing, improving, and smashing scoring barriers to reach new levels.

Grit and mental toughness became critical components on our journey.

As a golfer in the Pacific Northwest, grit is a critical asset when contending with unpredictable weather patterns in the spring and fall. During our traditional spring season, we never know if we are going to get: a Pineapple Express from Hawaii, with enormous wind gusts and pelting rain; or a bitterly cold storm pattern dropping down from Alaska. When the weather conditions are assaulting you, you either have to relax and move through it or decide that the climate is just not for you.

Note: If you are a potential recruit, learning how to play in some interesting weather conditions will only make you stronger and more successful!

Over the years, I saw grit in our players, but I also observed that young women can sell themselves short on what they think or believe they can achieve. My work as a coach has involved convincing them that they are capable of achieving far more than they ever thought possible.

One of the ways we have pushed ourselves to new heights is by following the Navy Seal 40 percent rule. The rule was first conceived by former Navy Seal David Goggin.[1] Basically, the term means that when your body and mind are feeling completely exhausted and you believe you have given your all and think you are done, you are only at 40 percent of what you are truly capable of doing. Your mind can be telling you, *I'm at my limit,* while your body is capable of reaching much higher thresholds.

IT AIN'T OVER 'TIL IT'S OVER

We had a player use this concept for the final round of a tournament. She had started off slowly with bogeys on her first five holes. She told me she felt both her mental and physical energy caving in after going all in during the first round the previous day. As her score crept higher, she started questioning if she had anything left to give for the final round. She told me that her mind was giving in to defeat—and thinking, *I just don't have it today.*

She was starting to defer to the negativity when she remembered her process goals: *be a warrior for the entire round* and *stay in the present.* She resumed trusting her process while exercising the Navy Seal 40 percent rule and taking it one shot at a time. She made a par, followed by a birdie, and then her adrenaline ramped up and she suddenly felt an inner superpower she had never experienced before. This dynamo shot 5-under for the next 13 holes and finished the tournament in third place after almost giving up. She attributed her turnaround to her mind convincing her that she had more to give, and she performed better than she ever thought was possible that day.

Since D-III student-athletes do not receive athletic scholarships, they may start out at a disadvantage over the players at D-I schools who have bigger facilities, budgets, and resources. D-III schools are not often invited to D-I tournaments for obvious reasons—a D-I school losing to a D-III school does not make a D-I coach look good or help them in the rankings.

So how can a D-III player overcome the handicap of playing for a smaller school and still pursue academics and golf at the highest level? It comes down to grit.

So far, we've had two players receive special exemptions to play in a LPGA tournament and two who qualified for the US Women's Amateur by actually winning the qualifying tournaments against mainly D-I players. Was it talent that won the day? I'd say sure, they're talented but the main differentiators were mental toughness and grit. My players refused to believe they were any less than anyone in the tournament—regardless of Division. They never gave up, even when they made a mistake. They persevered—regardless.

The D-III experience isn't any less than anything else. Anyone can work at improving their technical game and swing mechanics, but working hard to improve mindset and mental toughness in the face of challenge is where the game is won.

Courage and grit go hand-in-hand. Competitors decide their mindset and their determination level. Of course, fear will tempt you to say, "I don't have it today" or "I don't have the energy to do it." Succumbing to fear might seem easier than battling on. Then, there's also the ego, which, when driven by fear, might try to keep you from looking bad and say, "You don't have to play today—wouldn't that be better than losing?" You get to choose which voice you listen to.

Mental Toughness Training Tip:

Getting to the top of the podium is not just about recruiting talent; it's about recruiting passion and grit! Players need to be willing to do what needs to be done when the pressure is on. To be successful, you must commit to being all in and to playing with fortitude and tenacity.

Tim Grover, the former coach for Michael Jordan and Kobe Bryant says, "Winning makes you different and different scares people!"[2] I sensed that as our team became more successful. As we achieved more, there seemed to be more adverse challenges we had to maneuver around.

At one tournament, I was faced with a difficult rules' situation at a coach's meeting the night before Day One of our Conference Championship. A coach had set up a local rule on one of the shorter par 4 holes which had a penalty area in front of the green. A drop zone was added on the other side of the penalty area/water next to the green that would be used if a player hit it into the water—adding one stroke to their score.

This new local rule confounded me because it didn't seem fair—it basically allowed a player to hit their tee shot into the water hazard/penalty area, take their one stroke penalty, and move their ball to the other side right next to the green, drop it, and still be chipping for birdie. The integrity of how the hole was meant to be played—and strategized—was jeopardized. However, the coaches disagreed with my questioning of the rule and voted to let it stand.

Later that night back in my hotel room, I continued to stew about the local rule. I was too hyper to even think about sleep, so I opened my laptop to research such a ruling and a possible answer.

I WON'T BACK DOWN

A note that I had given the team popped out at me from my desktop window. The note was an affirmation—*Trust you. Be you.* A sign? Being a people pleaser, it can be a difficult task trying to keep everyone happy *and* trusting yourself.

Mental Toughness Training Tip:

It's important to be who you are and not let what others might think of you sway you off course. Others can help guide you, but success comes from within you.

I think I finally relaxed when I saw those words. My cortisol level dropped, and my mind suddenly felt clearer.

I remembered that I had a friend who is a national USGA rules official —so I sent her an email to tap her expertise on the matter. I knew she could at least explain if we were following the rules correctly, and I would have some clarity about this distracting rule.

When I woke up the next morning, I had received a text from my friend. I couldn't believe the news! She had already contacted our Conference Championship rules official and alerted him to the rule situation. Unbeknownst to me, she knew the rules official for our tournament.

The rules official had not seen the drop zone location when he approved the rule change. He actually went out early that morning to check and saw that it was on the wrong side of the water/penalty area and moved it back to the fairway side. In essence, he agreed that move was required in order to follow USGA rules.

I could not believe what I was reading. The local rule we had voted on was eliminated. I could feel my heart beating faster as I thought, *What are the coaches going to think now?*

When I arrived at the course with the team, I knew immediately that word had already spread that the local rule was not being allowed. I even overheard a coach on the range say to another coach "She is beyond gutsy." I knew he was referring to me, but what had I done wrong in checking on a rule that seemed completely illegitimate?

The rules official stood his ground and informed everyone that he could not govern the tournament if our conference did not follow USGA guidelines. I was relieved that we were following the rules but completely saddened by all the drama that was transpiring. I felt like the bad guy (bad *gal* in my case!) who challenged the rule only to protect our team—which was not the case. But then, yes, our team won the tournament, so it was quite easy for everyone to believe that's what had happened.

Following play, a luncheon was held for all the players and coaches in a large meeting space inside the clubhouse. Even though our team had legitimately won the event, there were no congratulations or niceties exchanged.

I was one of the last to arrive at the lunch area and was walking through the maze of tables to get to our team, when a player from another team approached me. She asked me if we had won the tournament. When I said yes, she initially said that she wanted to thank me personally. My heart leapt for a split second when I thought another player was happy about the official rule change. Boy, was I off base! She followed the thank you by saying, "Because of you, I scored a big number on the 8th hole today and had one of the worst rounds of my life." Her coach had told her that I was responsible, so she wanted to make sure I knew how devastated she was feeling.

Huh? I couldn't believe what she was saying, and that she was blaming me. I didn't know what to say. I wanted to somehow take away her suffering and make it better. I told her it was the rules official who had made the decision based on USGA guidelines and not me. She nevertheless rolled her eyes, glared at me some more, then turned and stomped away without saying another word.

I couldn't take my eyes off her as she walked away. My heart sank and tears welled in my eyes. I was truly devastated by her pain along with this misinformation and ugly spirit clouding the room. *I must do better to help these young women find their greatness,* I thought to myself.

My heart hurt for that misguided player but also for the coach who seemed to want me to feel responsible. I wiped my tears and joined our team for lunch. My intention was never to make any hole more difficult, wish that any player would have a bad round or cause friction with the other coaches. I was just trying to do the right thing—stand up for the rules for all the tournament players. No team had a leg up because of the rule change.

GET UP, STAND UP

It was in that sad moment I decided I had to tell this story. No one will believe this. No one will believe some of barriers and even hostility I feel at times for standing up for the right thing and then experiencing how it can get so twisted.

Would that coach have sent her player over to confront me if I had been a man or a PGA member? I do not know the answer. But what I have learned is that sometimes deciding to do the right thing causes pain when others around you disagree. I had no idea how other players would emotionally respond. I simply wanted to check on this ruling and make sure we were following it correctly.

About a week after the Championship, I heard that one of the coaches had filed a complaint with the commissioner suggesting that I had interfered with a ruling approved by the majority of the coaches at the tournament. The commissioner responded that if the rules official had not changed the local rule back to follow the USGA rules, the tournament would have been moot, cancelled, no good. The NCAA would not have accepted our Conference Championship as a legitimate tournament, nor would scores have counted toward the conference or Nationals.

On one hand I was proud that I knew that USGA rule and had the guts to challenge it, but on the other hand, I felt bad that some players and coaches were so completely distraught.

Then I remembered a former player who had been disqualified at a tournament for a rule infraction five years earlier. I will never forget the painful look on her face when she was *not* selected as an All-American at the National awards banquet after having an absolutely outstanding season her senior year. Since she'd been disqualified, she finished last rather than in second place at that tournament. It was that disqualification that hurt her from being named to the All-American team. It was an entirely different rule situation, but it reinforced that knowing the rules and following the rules is extremely important. I would not be shamed into thinking differently.

Mental Toughness Training Tip:

Arriving in the arena is a challenge but staying there is even harder. Grit and courage are required especially during challenges. It's not always going to feel good. Keep the bigger picture in mind and listen to your heart.

Our team learned a lot that weekend and earned an invitation to the National Championship as underdogs that year. We came super close to winning the whole thing during the final round, but thunderstorms rolled in holding up play. We had been tied for third going into the final 18 holes but had moved into second place and were closing in on first, when the horn blew to stop play due to lightning.

Under that dark Texas sky, we headed for cover where we waited and waited for the lightning to pass. But alas, the storm continued and eventually the NCAA made the call that we had run out of time to finish our final round. The Championship would stand with how things stood after three rounds, which meant we tied for third.

Could we have climbed to the top that day? We were on our way, but we will never know. What we do know, is that our grit is how we got there.

Special Nugget for When Girls Win!

When Girls Win, we know that intimidating tactics will be used against us, but we keep our heads up, avoid emotion so we can think clearly, and persevere. Worrying about what others think will not get the job done or help you succeed. Stay true to your values and do the right thing. If others think less of you, know that is their problem, not yours.

As women coaches, we also know that in a male-dominated sport like golf, we will have difficulty earning status and respect. *When Girls Win*, we compete anyway and know we deserve to be there. We embody grit and courage and stay true to ourselves and our passion. We strive for excellence, take on the challenges in a positive way and understand that some people will judge us when we speak the truth.

I'VE GOT TO USE MY IMAGINATION

I don't run away from a challenge because I am afraid. Instead, I run toward it because the only way to escape fear is to trample it beneath your feet.

–Nadia Comăneci, Olympic Gold Medalist, Romania Gymnastics

"Wow, you have the opportunity to create a successful program —or not," said my wise New York friend when I told him about my new coaching job. He had been a quarterback at Yale and a big follower of various championship sports teams over the years. Basically, he was saying, "Win or lose, this is all on you!"

Yikes, I hadn't really thought about it that way until he said those words. "Of course, I want to start a successful team," I answered back. He continued that it was evident from watching so many different sports teams over the years that if I didn't get it going in the right direction from the start it might take a very long time to swing it in the right direction. Pun intended! Nothing like feeling pressure right out of the gate!

His words actually made me realize that I needed to think outside the box in order to do what seemed impossible. As I've discussed, in the Pacific Northwest, we had weather against us—and no indoor practice facility. We had no athletic scholarships in this division—nor would we ever. We had no established or ranked team yet to draw eager recruits. We had conference opponents whose teams had existed for years and longtime seasoned men's teams and coaches, but the women's teams were still developing. In our region, we would be up against established top teams in sunshine states like California and Texas.

I kept thinking, if we can overcome all those obstacles, we have a chance.

Some of my learning has come from people not associated with the golf industry or even in sports. One of those individuals is marketing and advertising guru and author, Seth Godin. In his book, *This is Marketing*, he says that "Success comes from finding a creative solution to our problems. No matter what."[1] Thus, my job became to find creative solutions to all the barriers we had stacked against us. I also had to anticipate new potential roadblocks and hurdles that would inevitably pop up. I had to keep an open mind and think differently.

My background is in marketing, so I knew that expertise would play a role in our journey to both attract great recruits and attract outside support. We had to create a culture and program that other people wanted to be a part of—and that would bring attention to our team. We had to be creative in everything we did from cool uniforms and innovative mental toughness training to decent practice facilities, challenging practices, and setting up a great travel schedule outside the Pacific Northwest with opportunities to play excellent golf courses.

DREAM ON

I knew the dream of becoming a national championship team would be a Mt. Everest-style mission, but I also knew if our team could stay passionate, motivated, dedicate themselves, and make it a gradual climb, we could quite possibly make our way to the summit.

We added a tournament in Phoenix right out of the gate. We jazzed up our golf bags and uniforms. We turned our school color of gold into Nike neon yellow–a bold attention grab, so our team stood out on the links. We even bought cool shoes! Then, I began the task of fundraising for an indoor practice center to use during inclement weather. No small feat to be sure.

We had to be innovative to find creative solutions for every aspect of building this team—that energized me, and the team was feeling it, too. We thrived on the creativity.

Did we feel the resistance as we were growing as a team? You bet! All the time. And then my own negative thoughts start to haunt me: *This is too hard. You are never going to raise enough money to take your team to Notre Dame. The indoor center looks great on paper, but you're $40k short.*

Again, remember the quote by Steven Pressfield in *The War of Art*, "The danger (of resistance) is greatest when the finish line is in sight."[2] He's talking about writing, but I believe it applies to everything. Resistance exists—it always will. But when you realize there are creative solutions to jump the hurdles, and you learn to visualize success and outcomes, release self-sabotage and self-doubt, you can make the impossible happen.

"Obstacles do not have to stop you. If you run into a wall, don't turn around and give up. Figure out how to climb it, go through it, or work around it," says legendary athlete Michael Jordan.[3]

Inventively maneuvering around the inevitable roadblocks was key to our breakthroughs. Seth is right. Change does create tension, but it's the only way to shake up the status quo and succeed.

Mental Toughness Training Tip:

There is always a way around resistance. Remember the Navy Seal 40 percent rule? Even when you feel like quitting, just know you are closer to a breakthrough than you think. Winners breathe, learn, let go and keep going.

SUDDENLY I SEE

Over the years I've heard some pretty interesting rationale from players justifying their poor performance: The course didn't fit my game today; the greens were in terrible condition; the pins were unfair; the weather sucked; a player in my group was rude and never stopped talking; no one cheered for me on purpose; my group was put on the clock, and it messed up my rhythm."

And of course, the winner: It's the coach's fault.

One of the key lessons I've learned as a coach—and in life—is that if your intention is to rise to a higher level, then you must *take responsibility*. Period.

Own your play.

Players who take responsibility are champion-minded and distinguish themselves from the blamers. They are quicker to achieve elite status because they take an inner look at themselves and understand what they can do differently next time. They exude a level of self-awareness that others have not yet attained. Taking responsibility, learning from mistakes, and simply observing yourself and your patterns goes a long way to advancement.

Mental Toughness Training Tip:

Take responsibility for your mistakes. Take responsibility for the attitude you bring to your game. Take responsibility for how you treat your teammates and your coach. Take responsibility for your success with grateful-

ness and humility. Lose the ego-soaked excuses and you will excel much further in your sport and in life.

I admit it: Some of the excuses I used when I was young were perfectly ridiculous. I mean seriously! Once I even told my dad that I missed my putt because the greens mower stopped to watch me putt! It was his fault. Pathetic, no? My dad's comeback: "No, he was just hoping that you would stop taking so long, so he could finish mowing." I had such a hard time accepting my own mistakes. Hello—ego calling!

When I started competing in tournaments and didn't accomplish the outcome I'd expected, I complained and found excuses. Pointing the finger relieved my negative feelings that I just wasn't up-to-par—figuratively and literally!

One time, a close golfing friend listened with compassion, but then afterwards said, "Hey look, remember, nobody cares what your score is —they're too focused on their own game." She went on to explain that half of the players don't care if my score was high, and the other half wished I shot even higher. Those words stuck in my head and seemed so shocking, but it's true. I mean, I am not sure everyone hopes you play worse—but no one is really concerned about how you do.

If you are fortunate, you have close family and friends and possibly your team who are cheering you on, but other than that, why is the blame game so prevalent? I believe it's much easier to blame rather than deal with those ugly inner feelings—especially when you feel like you let yourself and your team down.

When your ego is shouting, "You are better than this," it can be painful to take responsibility. If you are perfectionist, it's even harder. Our egos are quite fragile and are based on fear. When we are not feeling good enough or successful enough or just not enough, it's hard to accept our own role in our meager performance—or the negative attitude that got us there.

And to add fuel to your fire, in golf, your score for the day is posted publicly next to your name on a huge tournament sign. Ouch! Especially if your score is not measuring up to the beliefs you have about yourself—and your play. Blame can storm into the picture when you feel inadequate and it's unbearable to accept your performance.

BLAME IT ON THE BOOGIE

As a new coach, I remember walking up to our team during the early years all huddled together following the final round of a tournament. I smiled as I approached because I thought they were cheering each other on and it warmed my heart. When I got closer, I realized that they were discussing a competitor saying things like, "She's just super cocky and hard to play with."

My heart stopped. Even if the competitor *was* cocky, putting that blame on another player, coach, parent, or condition does not enhance your reputation nor your ability. You might feel better in that moment, but that's about it. I was upset that they had chosen this path—and afterward, we enforced stricter team rules making discussion of other players or placing blame unacceptable.

Want a champion mindset? Then self-reflect on what *you* can do better. You cannot control how others behave or what attitude they bring to the competition, but you *can* control your own mindset and how you show up!

I must admit, sometimes it *is* the coach's fault. We don't always make the best decisions. We don't always know how a player is going to show up that day. We don't always say the right things. However, blaming the coach doesn't help either party improve. The coach is in a constant learning mode as well and if you have a good coach, she/he is wanting you to do well, just like a teacher.

If a player walks around saying, "The coach isn't putting me in the line-up because she/he doesn't like me or likes someone else better" than maybe that player should take a deeper dive and ask, "How can I show the coach that I deserve the opportunity?"

Limits originate in blame. Champions are those who take responsibility—and observe themselves in order to learn and advance.

While so many competitors are furiously searching for that secret swing key or the magic tip to catapult them to the top, it is taking responsibility that propels you faster than anything else. It is where we observe our behavior and own our play—and we improve our game.

It's not just performance—taking responsibility for your attitude is equally important. Bringing indomitable energy and attitude to your game are critical. As sports psychologist/guru Dr. Rotella says, "The biggest mistake players make is to let how they play dictate their attitude."[4]

Mental Toughness Training Tip:

Reminder again: Accept and take responsibility for mistakes. You MUST be stronger mentally than your strongest excuse.

Special Nugget for When Girls Win

When Girls Win, we take responsibility for our actions, learn from them, and understand more about how powerful we truly are. Taking responsibility is freedom from trying to hide our downfalls. We see through the excuses and witness our strength when we own our behavior and the mistakes we have made.

We find creative solutions. As Marie Forleo says in her book titled, *Everything is Figureaoutable,* "The power isn't out there, it's in you."[5] We dive deeper and find unique ways around the blockades. Giving in is not an option. We trust our own inner wisdom and hear the guidance speak to us. We rely on our own strength and trust in our good energy.

BLANK SPACE

I am building a fire, and every day I train, I add more fuel.
At just the right moment, I light the match.

–Mia Hamm, Olympic Gold Medalist, U.S. Soccer

Wait—so where have you heard this expression before? "Don't think, just do."

It's the simple but powerful mental toughness mantra that Maverick aka Tom Cruise uses in the *Top Gun: Maverick* movie, as he trains his Navy fighter pilot elite graduates. His job, to get his pilots on *cruise control* so they can accomplish their high-risk mission.

When we think too much about an action we have learned, our left brain is too slow to perform at the highest level. We are basically too conscious and not in the flow. According to author Ed Grant, "The conscious mind simply can't perform over-learned skills."[1] Grant says an experiment to try is an overlearned behavior like signing your name. Try signing your name like you normally do and then try thinking about your signature while tracing over the top of your first signature. It's hard to do it as quickly as you did it the first time when you were not thinking. Try it. We have learned to sign our names, and over time we just do it without any conscious thinking. We allow ourselves to let our innate ability and our right brain, subconscious brain, to take over.[1] We play our best when we *just do it*.

Think about learning to drive a car. We have trained behind the wheel —anticipating different conditions and situations and after a while we just unconsciously know what to do. We stop at a corner and press our foot on the brake without really thinking, "Now I must take my right foot and step down on the brake pad." We just do it. We have learned to drive, and our subconscious takes over. We are still aware of our surroundings, but we aren't *thinking* about each action like turning the steering wheel or turning on a turn signal, we just allow it to happen.

In *Top Gun: Maverick*, the top fighter pilots memorize and practice their dangerous missions via a training course and simulator. They glide over jagged mountain peaks and maneuver their aircrafts with precision through low narrow and curvy canyons at high rates of speed —to go after their target and then climb straight up and over another peak, dodging fierce retaliation in enemy territory.

Maverick told the elite pilots that to achieve their mission they had to practice hard and then visualize doing it. He demonstrated the mission via a practice course to show that it was possible to get to their target to help them feel and believe that success was possible. They physically learned the specific tactics of the mission and then had to trust, let go and do it without consciously thinking! They had to trust their instincts while flying their aircraft because if they started second-guessing their capabilities on this risky mission, they most likely would not come back alive. Maverick emphasizes, "Think up there, and you are dead." The ultimate mental test! Note: I was pumped to see a female fighter pilot as one of the elite pilots chosen!

Mental Toughness Training Tip:

Visualization and trust are vital components to staying in the moment and succeeding with the task at hand.

LET IT GO

I had a player who practiced her technical game in 30-minute blocks on the range every day. After she had completed her skill training, I'd come over and say, "See those two trees down the fairway about 30 yards apart? You are on the first hole at our next tournament, now hit your drive! She'd tee up her ball, go through her routine, look at her target visualizing and really feeling like she was on that first tee and *let it happen.* In competition, do the same—trust your instincts and *let it go!*

Keep your right elbow in. Keep your wrist bowed at the top. Pull down with your left shoulder. Get to your forward foot quickly. Keep your head down through the shot. Those might be a few physical techniques we would be practicing on the range, but all that chatter will only get in the way during competition and keep you from performing at your highest level. In my experience, it can be okay for a player to have one positive key swing thought for the pre-shot routine—but it should be limited to just one thought, or you will think too much and get in your own way. You won't die, but it won't be good.

My player worked on this process over and over of seeing her target and then letting go until she trusted it completely! When she found that ease of just doing it, she had some incredible scoring break-throughs and eventually went on to become our first NCAA National Player of the Year! I mean, wow! What a gift to witness when your hardworking player shifts it into *cruise control.*

I learned a lot in working with this player, as it helped me understand more about the absolute power of our subconscious mind. Basically, she was letting go of her left side thinking and used more of her right-side thinking. This allowed her to perform more subconsciously and without interference of mechanical thoughts, and/or the ego creeping in with self-doubt. Many times, we end up sabotaging ourselves and our ability to achieve becomes limited.

Mental Toughness Training Tip:

Once you feel confidence in your physical training, then rehearse letting it happen. Don't think, just do! Like the line in Caddyshack: *"Be the ball."*

Our team recently had a player earn a spot in the US Women's Amateur. Of course, she was super excited about the opportunity to play against the very best women amateurs. She had worked really hard on both her physical game and her inner game and felt ready for the challenge. But she got off to a slow start with bogeys and over par rounds in the first 27 holes of stroke play—not nearly as good as her scoring average.

On her final 9 holes to make the cut for match play, she was on fire and shot 2-under par. I asked her afterwards what ignited her on the last nine. "I finally accepted my game, and I just played," she replied.

Whoa! As her coach, I thought to myself, "Umm, why didn't we start out that way?" However, the pressure of being on stage in the big moment had made her think that she needed to do something different than how she had been playing. Add to that, this was a unique links-style course with massive greens and bunkers—causing her to strategize a little more and try a little harder to compete rather than to just play and let go.

Mental Toughness Training Tip:

Trust more and do less. Sometimes in more competitive situations we think we need to do more, be more, when we just need to trust more and be more accepting. That is true inner toughness right there.

JUST BREATHE

One of the biggest mental mistakes we deal with is when we're really going for the win—we know we've worked hard, dedicated ourselves and deserve it. But when we try to control the outcome—wrestle it to the ground—the left brain or conscious mind interferes with the flow, and BAM, we find ourselves in an overthinking sinking ship and we fail.

As Kevin Costner's character says to Tim Robbins in the movie *Bull Durham:* "Don't think. It'll only hurt the ball club."

In the end, our only control is relaxing into the present moment! That's where our true power lies—the here and now. When it's go-time, *just go.* Period.

I must admit, I often tried too hard when I competed as a player because I wanted to win so badly! I remember a former PGA tour pro telling me that it was going to be impossible for me to get where I wanted to go because I wanted it too badly. I asked him "What does that mean? Wanting it means you are driven, you are committed, you are going to outwork everyone."

"But wanting it too badly means *forcing, trying too hard, hoping, wishing, fearing you can't get what you want and trying to control things* that are out of your control," he responded.

Here I had always thought that if my mind and body were battling for it, I would have a greater chance of getting it. I struggled with finding the zone because I had a constant battle going on between my conscious mind—my ego and controlling side–and my subconscious, my innate ability to do my thing and flow. It's inner harmony that wins the day—not a constant inner battle.

There can be some confusion with the words *free* and *let go!* Not that long ago, I told one member of our team to *let go and just be free* on the course at a tournament. During our team talk, I emphasized being free from fear and worry, free from swing thoughts. I told them to *just play and let it happen.* Well, the word *free* worked for some that day, but others went a little too extreme, lost focus and had a *free-for-all!*

So, how do you *just let go* or *just do* without losing the important concentration piece required? Your mind can't be left to just wander or you will have a hard time focusing. An important key to master is how to focus while also staying relaxed. That's the place where the zone can find you. Your mind is focused and concentrating on the task at hand without succumbing to thinking about it (like signing your name) and slowing you down.

Meditation is one of the best training tools you can do to help you learn to be in this focused cruise control place. It teaches you to come back to your breath and be in the moment. I know, it's not easy. Many of us can't sit still enough for even 10 minutes of meditation without our monkey minds luring us away to our to do lists. But it's about learning to notice your breath and even your wandering mind. Eventually, it helps you become more self-aware and in the present moment.

Mindfulness works as well. Pay attention to small things like washing your hands, sipping your coffee, chopping veggies—just being more present while engaged in activities. When you are eating, notice the taste and smells. Be in those moments. We are so used to multi-tasking and doing 20 things at once, but if we can return to centering ourselves in the present—we will eventually increase our concentration capabilities.

BE HERE NOW

Our team has worked on mindfulness practice as part of our process goals—we'll write down a score after each hole but not record it in our minds. Several players have learned to break scoring barriers by letting go of score. Just *one shot at a time* and *one hole at a time* are our ongoing mantras. On several occasions when players said they didn't know what they shot, they came in with under par rounds, and one tied the course record. Even at the 2022 National Championship, we had a player tie for the individual medal after the final round—she lost in a sudden death playoff, but she had no idea what her score was for the day or that she had caught the leader. She was focused on the moment, not on results.

Finally, if you judge your day by how you're hitting on the range, or if you judge yourself on a putt you missed on the 1st hole, you need to go back and start again at Chapter 1. Remember it's not the plane, it's the pilot!

Mental Toughness Training Tip:

No judging yourself while you are competing! The only focus should be staying with your process and watching the progress happen.

Self-limiting beliefs are robbers. Say you're having a magical day, clicking along, and shooting lights out—but many times, it almost feels like it's too good to be true, so we hit the brakes in order to try to hold on to the magic moments rather than stepping on the gas and going for it! Part of us does not believe we are capable of achieving more, so we resist, hold back and our subconscious gives us what it thinks we're striving for—our normal scoring range.

But here's some good news: You can learn how to break through scoring barriers by understanding that *you* cause those limits. As you keep expanding both your mental toolbox and your physical skills, you can push past those limits.

I know it's possible—I've done it and I've seen my players do it. The average player out there is not improving because they haven't worked hard on their inner/mental game. They go to the range, pound some balls, and believe they've improved. Of course, physical ability is important, but better results come by improving mental toughness skills.

This process of building confidence and "Don't think, just do" is something we continue to work on as a team. (Shoot! You're learning all our secrets!) It is a competitive advantage, our secret sauce—and the work has paid off. In 2021, we had a player at the top of the leaderboard at the National Championship all week who stayed in her own zone, unphased and just doing her thing, and she went on to win by 14 strokes over the field, becoming a National Champion. In 2022, we had another player in the top 5 all week and then during the last round, she tied for the lowest individual score only to lose to an amazing birdie by her competitor—still, she became National Runner Up.

These players ability to *let it happen* under pressure have been true *Top Gun* moments. Don't think, just do.

There's a great interview with PGA tour pro, Max Homa after he shot 62 at the FedEx Cup in 2022: "I had to say to myself, 'Why are you putting so much pressure on yourself. Just let yourself go do something good.' I felt FREE to play and TRUSTED that I was good at golf. Sometimes I don't believe that. So, I walked around like I believed it. I work really, really hard and if I don't see results then I think what's the point. Golf will test your *brain,* and I felt like I deserved to play well, but I wasn't *letting myself* play well. Trust that you put in the work."[2]

Mental Toughness Training Tip:

Letting it happen subconsciously means that you are executing your task with a clear, focused and trusting mindset. The more trust and belief you have in yourself, the more you will be free from control of the conscious mind.

Special Nugget for When Girls Win:

When Girls Win, we understand that we can overthink things and try too hard. We free ourselves from focusing on perfection and do the best we can. We worry less about ideal results and just try to win each moment/day with grateful hearts and trust.

I WILL SURVIVE

You have to believe in yourself when no one else does.

–Serena Williams, Tennis Champion

The year: 2017. Our team is ranked #1 in the country for the entire season—fall through spring. As we arrive at the National Championship in May we are officially known as *the team to beat.* This is the dream goal. This is exactly where we want to be. This is the mission and vision we set for ourselves when launching the program.

We've accomplished a momentous feat—and it feels a little daunting! But let's be clear—it's just a ranking. Now the pressure is on to prove that the ranking got it right.

There's some nervousness but also pure excitement as we land in Houston. We step off the plane into the hot, humid air and brace for the sweltering heat of midday in Texas. We are prepared this time. We are proud of our standing—even team-to-beat targets on our backs. We confidently walk down the country club entryway dotted with big round NCAA Championship logos toward the NCAA registration area. We feel comfortable and ready.

We pick up our registration packets and head over to the putting green. I am grabbing some water at a nearby cooler and happen to overhear a competitor whisper and point to her teammate: "That's who we need to beat." I get goose bumps. The other player responds, "Can they be that good when they are from Oregon?" Now, I'm standing taller and adamant, *Yes, they can!* I thought. Not to sound overconfident here, but I walked away, knowing in my heart that our team was on a mission, exuding an unstoppable vibe. We were embracing the pressure, the expectations, and the anticipation of competition.

Mental Toughness Training Tip:

Embrace the pressure! Accept nerves and remind yourself that excitement is good. Nerves mean you are ready.

In all sports, and particularly golf, surprises happen. Situations you'd least expect—things that just don't happen when you practice or are just out playing with teammates seem to materialize out of nowhere. Your golf ball can kick off an obstruction and land behind a tree. Your ball can get plugged in a divot or a bunker. You just don't know when you might receive an unlucky break or bounce. It's so easy to panic in these unusual situations or get emotional about the unfair bad break. But those pity parties can often lead to a potential blow-up hole and kill what might have been a good score.

As our team learned to accept the surprise situations, and how to play smarter through them, they also learned to stay patient and accept whatever happens. They quickly let go—knowing they can still make up ground with the right mindset.

I pride myself on preparing our team for surprises—and practicing recovering from an errant shot. Besides the physical skill like hitting out of a deep divot, mentally rehearsing is crucial as well. The brain doesn't know the difference between real and rehearsal, so if you can set up unusual situations during practice, you will feel calmer and prepared when surprises arise.

The mental rehearsal is critically important because we absolutely cannot foresee or prepare for everything. Our team has definitely had its share of crazy surprises. One was a 2 a.m. fire alarm during a National Championship at a remote resort in Central Florida. We had to evacuate our building and waited two-and-a-half hours for an *all clear* from the volunteer fire department before we could go back in. Although it was nice and warm out for the entire wait time, when we got back to our rooms, we literally had just 45 more minutes to sleep before our alarms would buzz to prepare for 7 a.m. tee times. Ouch!

Another total surprise was witnessing the head of a player's driver fly down the range when she was warming up prior to a practice round at a big tournament at Notre Dame. Her club was damaged on the flight and the next she knew her driver head had shot down the range about 50 yards. Then there's the coach racing to help a player in trouble and accidentally getting stuck in a brutal waste area bunker. Ooooops! If you are mentally prepared to anticipate and react to all the unexpected things that arise, you will be way ahead of the game.

Mental Toughness Training Tip:

Think about potential surprises before your competition and visualize yourself handling them with a calm and confident attitude.

When surprised, emotions arise, and as mentioned earlier, cortisol levels go up and we arrive in that perplexed what-do-I-do-now dilemma. "Surprise leads to emotion and in this game, it will kill you," says Johnny in David Cook's *Seven Days in Utopia: Golf's Sacred Journey.*[1] Prepare! Rehearse! Anticipate!

Even with all the pressure on my players, they played the first three rounds relaxed, confident and driven. We owned the number one position as a team and knew we had earned the spot. We felt comfortable just doing our thing—following our routine and process each morning.

After three rounds, we were in the lead by 2 strokes. In fact, we had an amazing third round and shot the lowest one-day score of any other team that day to show that we meant business. We felt prepared for anything, and we couldn't wait for that final round!

As I always do, I checked the weather the night before the final round, and it looked like the late spring Texas thunderstorms wouldn't threaten play until later in the day. Weather conditions can create some of the biggest surprises for golfers. We learned our lesson once when we didn't anticipate rain and lost because we weren't prepared for the soggy conditions.

RIDE LIKE THE WIND

When we arrived at the course for the final round, I noticed that the flags representing all the schools near the 18th green were flapping a little differently than they had been on the last three days. I didn't think much of it initially, as there wasn't much of a breeze, but as our warm-up continued, the wind gained momentum and by the time we teed off, the flags were blowing in the exact opposite direction.

Hmmmmm. Something's brewing.

During our team meeting that morning, I noted to our players to pay attention to wind direction, but I also didn't want them to *overthink it.* They were in a great energy place and I wanted them to stay there and to let it go.

Joe Skovron, the former longtime caddie for PGA tour pro, Rickie Fowler, once spoke at our National Golf Coaches convention, and emphasized the biggest difference between great amateurs and a tour pro is the ability to play in the wind and confidently revise a shot strategy instantly when the wind shifts. He said that amateurs tend to underestimate the power of the wind and how it affects all phases of their game.

Right from the get-go, the wind was requiring us to adjust our shots and especially target lines, but the players kept playing with confidence as it appeared that nothing was going to get in their way. We were playing our game, hitting our same clubs, and were able to adapt to the wind. Our advantage for the first three rounds had been our tee shots. We had been able to take advantage of the par 5s and the long par 4s all week. However, when the wind shifted in the opposite direction, the drives on the downwind holes were going way too far and getting our players in trouble.

How do you remain confident and committed when you need to adjust your clubs, your swing, your game? For the entire tournament, the players had been trusting their game plan and strategy and felt comfortable, especially off the tee. On the back 9, which was the more strategic 9, we had to quickly adapt to the turbulent wind gusts that were wreaking some serious havoc.

Our team handled all the little surprises, but now we had to hit different clubs from almost every tee box and in some cases that meant hitting an iron instead of a driver. Of course, all competitors were in this same situation, so it became a battle of choosing the right club and shifting gears to a new strategy hole-by-hole—and all with a confident mindset. We came very close to pulling it off, but in the end, fell 2 strokes short.

I am certainly not blaming the wind. Everyone had to deal with it and for the most part, the scores were higher for almost everyone that final round. We learned how important it is to adapt our mindset and game plan in the middle of a competition when a surprise like a dramatic wind shift hits. We could still hit the shots, but our confidence did not quite match up.

We emerged as the National Runner-up which still felt like a phenomenal achievement. We were right there. We showed everyone that we belonged on the National stage. Sometimes, it is just a matter of inches between first and second. If two more putts had fallen, we would have been in a playoff. It was that close! It's amazing to me that with teams scoring a total around 1,200 strokes (4 out of 5 scores per day) after 4 rounds that it can get down to a slim stroke or two.

Our finish stung. We were so close. We weren't feeling quite ready for dinner, so after the awards ceremony we decided to stop for frozen yogurt on the way back to the hotel. It was just our team alone in the van, not ready to listen to music, quietly thinking about the day and the *if only's*. We achieved so much over the season, but the team was not ready to hear that. We were disappointed. My phone buzzed with a text from a great coaching colleague and mentor: "There are no words." And in that moment, I believed her.

GOT TO BE REAL

Once inside the frozen yogurt shop, I was thinking about how I could rally everyone back to a higher vibe. It had been such an incredible season. So many times, in so many sports, it gets down to a matter of those last few seconds of play or even overtime. That is what makes sports so exciting—those nail-biting finishes when you just don't know which way it will end. This was one of them.

I am not into participation awards, but I am into participation! Only one team—out of 30 qualified teams—can win the trophy. But competing, being in that national arena and dealing with all the surprises, is a valuable life lesson that will make you better all around.

All our players were silently sampling various yogurt flavors, but no one was speaking. Leave it to me to get the handle on one of the machines stuck. My little sample cup of swirl quickly overflowed with yogurt sliding down my hand and onto the floor. I shrieked at everyone to help me shut the machine off. Frozen yogurt had also attacked my golf skort, and everyone was doubled over in laughter! I was relieved to break the ice for the team—and hopefully not the machine!

In that crazy frozen yogurt moment, I knew we would all be fine. In fact, Mick Jagger added to our mood rebound when one of his hit songs blasted over the speakers in the shop as we were cleaning up the mess, "You can't always get what you want, but you get what you need."

Mental Toughness Training Tip:

Showing up in the arena is a big part of growth. Surprises will happen, and how we deal with them is the real test. Laughing after you fought through them is pure joy.

Our team had so much love and joy for each other and for what we'd just been through. We were all so grateful for what we had accomplished. We were so proud of giving it our all and doing our best! We had no regrets. In the end, we may not have officially been the National Champions, but we walked away as true champions in our hearts—and that is all that matters.

Mental Toughness Training Tip:

Giving your best is knowing that you did everything you could. Having no regrets is fine as long as you learned from the experience. Celebrate the small wins as that will help motivate your subconscious mind in the future.

Special Nugget for When Girls Win!

When Girls Win, we are ready for surprises because we know that being able to shift gears quickly is important both on and off the course. We celebrate our wins—no matter what—and keep marching on as we know more wins are in our future!

NOT ALL HEROES WEAR CAPES

Make it a point to be around those with positive energy – people who
want what's best for you, people who understand
your goals and priorities.

–Rebecca Lobo, former WNBA basketball player, current TV analyst

I will never forget the day I met LPGA Hall of Fame Coach, Linda Vollstedt. She was invited to speak at our Women's Golf Coaches Association annual convention in Las Vegas. The convention is held every December for coaches in all NCAA divisions and NAIA coaches in conjunction with the men's Golf Coaches of America Association annual convention. Many of the men's and women's golf coaching sessions overlap, but this particular session was for WGCA members only.

I had heard about Coach LV and her tremendous success (six NCAA National Championships) as the Head Women's Golf Coach at Arizona State University for 21 years (1980-2001) but had never met her or heard her speak before. We were in a large conference room in Planet

Hollywood with roundtable seating and a large stage with a podium and microphone. I was seated toward the back near the door.

When Coach LV walked in with a few other coaches, she was looking around and waving enthusiastically at those she knew in the room. I was very excited and sat up extra tall in my seat. She passed by my table as she continued to smile and wave at others. Then she looked right at me and said, "You have good energy, keep it up!" I turned a little red as I didn't expect her to look my way, let alone make a comment. I was relieved to hear that I was exuding positive energy, though. She continued her exuberant entrance then headed up to the stage and podium.

I sat there taking thorough notes while immersed in her words of experience and wisdom. I was completely captivated by her spirited energy filling the room, and I was eager to learn as much as possible. Before her arrival, I overheard several coaches mention that they felt like taking a nap after a long morning of sessions and a big lunch. Coach LV quickly conquered the sluggish energy in the room and captured our attention. My competitive side was hoping that some of my rival coaches might doze off and not pay attention, but darn it, everyone seemed to be hyper-focused on what Coach LV had to say.

The biggest thing I learned from Coach LV that day is how important your energy is. If you are feeling down about your performance or your team's performance, you are going to get more of it. Her message was simply: "The Universe is listening." What you put out there is what you get back.

So, if you are dragging yourself out of bed, hoping to do well, but dreading doing poorly, guess what? Most likely you will do poorly. That energy is everything. If you arrive in the van ready to go, ready to bring it the Universe conspires with you.

Following Coach LV's motivational talk, she and a few other big-name coaches led a breakout session going table-to-table to engage us in coaching tips. After a few rotations, Coach LV was at my table. We only had 15 minutes, but I hung on to every word as if I had discovered gold. Some coaches gave the impression they had it all down, but I was not missing a beat to learn from this six-time National Championship coach.

Mental Toughness Training Tip:

Remember the great Zen master, Shunryu Suzuki quote, "In the beginner's mind, there are many possibilities, but an expert's, there are few."[1] Always be open-minded, study those who excel and are at the top in your field and look for ways to improve and grow.

YOU'VE GOT A FRIEND

Many coaches and players make a big mistake in not following this tip very well. I have heard some coaches and other business professionals say they do not believe in mentors: "Who needs mentors when I have a trusted friend or family member in my camp?"

That sounds ego-driven. Is it a case of being a know-it-all and believing you have all the power? Or is it the fear that you'll look incompetent seeking the advice of others? When we think we have it all figured out, we close the door on learning from others' wisdom and experience. If you think you have it all figured out, no matter how much experience you have, you should really think again.

I've learned that we are all teachers *and* students. Read that again—out loud.

Engaging trusted mentors and an inner circle is critical to accelerating your growth and reaching new heights. If you only listen to what you want to hear and think you know it all, how do you leave your comfort zone, grow, and advance? How do you break through barriers if you can't handle constructive criticism or seek new insights on how to do something better?

As for me, I wanted to fully immerse in the wisdom, experience, and learnings of this six-time National Champ. Maybe she can help me achieve more!

I have always sought out mentors, both men and women. In fact, when I first started at the university in a smaller town in Oregon, I chatted a lot with another colleague who was then the Head Women's Basketball Coach. He coached one of the top basketball programs not only in our conference, but in the country, and I wanted to learn whatever I could from him on what it was going to take to succeed. He gave me a lot of excellent advice, and three years later, his team went on to enjoy an undefeated season and win the NCAA National Championship. He went on to develop a top D-I Women's Basketball program at another school in Oregon. I feel proud that this coach is still a mentor and I am still learning incredible tips from him.

I felt an immediate connection with Coach LV, and I was inspired and motivated by everything she had to say. Now the important question was whether I would be gutsy enough to ask her for advice in the future.

As the mentor breakout session was concluding, I raced over to get in line to chat with Coach LV. Many coaches were doing the same thing, so I just stood patiently waiting for a turn. I didn't even know what I was going to say, but I knew it was important to have a few moments of one-on-one time with her.

When I got to the front of the line, I introduced myself, and asked a general question about recruiting and what she looked for in players. I then surprised myself when I blurted out another question, asking if she would be willing to give me mentoring advice in the future. The words rushed out before I really had a chance to think it through. I could feel my face flush as I became a little embarrassed by my gumption. I assumed—incorrectly—that she might save her time advising coaches at bigger schools. Instead, she looked me in the eye and said she would be happy to talk to me and to email her. I wrote down her email and said that I would be in touch. I was thrilled that a new doorway was opening!

Mental Toughness Training Tip:

Build your power circle with people who will be truthful and tell you what you need to hear in order to improve. These are not people who always tell you what you want to hear–rather, people you trust to guide and inspire you. If you only listen to your family or a few close friends, you are likely just scratching the surface of knowledge that is available to you.

Over the past several years, I can proudly say that Coach LV has provided me with an unbelievable amount of guidance and support. It is no secret that she has offered countless suggestions and helped me tremendously. I am proud of myself for having the courage to reach out and for her invaluable insights.

HELP! I NEED SOMEBODY!

It's true—it takes a village! It really does. As Coach LV and I continued to work together, I realized that often I already knew the answer—it was inside of me. Knowing that my intuition was tuned in and that I was on the right path helped improve my confidence and become a stronger, more formidable coach. She also helped me understand that sometimes you have to *noodle* things, digest what you know, and wait for solutions to arise rather than instantly responding.

As coaches, sometimes we are anxious to make a decision—we want to ensure that win, we want success, we want to ensure we have the right line-up. However, most often, taking a deep breath and a step back to *noodle* the situation gets you to the very best decision. She has taught me to slow down during challenging times, to breathe in more confidence, trust my intuition and embrace great energy.

Coach LV's incredible experience, insight and gifts have been invaluable to my growth as a coach and as a person. Sometimes we need to see situations from another perspective. Sometimes we get caught making mountains out of molehills and we need a mentor to shed a little light. Of course, we're not going to run to someone for every decision but knowing you have support for the more challenging situations and difficult decisions is an incredible gift that leads to greater success.

Mental Toughness Training Tip:

Release ego and a need to control. Realize all the resources are available to you. The know-it-alls lose! Find honest advisors or books that can help you with your answers and needs. Ask questions. Seek mentors. Learn and grow from them. That's the name of the game.

I've been blessed with incredible teachers along my journey including Coach Mary Lou Mulflur from the University of Washington; Coach Paulette Pera from University of California at Santa Cruz; and Coach Kailin Downs at Boise State; all playing pivotal roles in my power circle, and I can't thank them enough!

I have three former players, two who are PGA members and business executives, Abby Mann, and Kelsey Smith, and also Madison Perry, a sports marketing guru, who have given me a lot of advice and different perspectives along the way. PGA Pro Brian Henninger and golf mental training coach, David Mackensie, have also helped me achieve *aha moments* that have made a profound difference.

Last, but certainly not least, I have found incredible inspiration from our University President Robin Baker, former Portland General Electric CEO Peggy Fowler, and entrepreneur Debra Phillips. I'd be remiss not to give a hearty shoutout to both of my older brothers and younger sister who are all successful in their own right—and have supported me on this path.

As players, you also need a circle of people who you can trust and have your best interest at heart. As players excel and rise in their fame many people want to jump on board to be part of that success. Be sure to protect your circle and manage unsolicited advice that may start flooding your way.

I am not at all about using every tip you hear on the range! No. Not the point. There are a million 12-handicappers on the range willing to give out free tips. I'm talking about listening to those whose expertise and wise guidance will continue helping you to grow.

Famous teaching professional Butch Harmon was at the same coaches convention the year I met Coach LV. He said some great things, but one thing struck me that was very powerful: "Keep an open mind. What you learn after you think you know it all will be the keys to your life!"[2]

Even Reese Witherspoon said recently on a TED podcast, "I would rather be a learn-it-all than a know-it-all."[3]

Think about it. If your ego gets too big, and you think you know it all, you will *not* embrace change and the lessons that lead you to success. My mentors have helped me achieve more than I even thought possible. In the end, we are all in it together.

Mental Toughness Training Tip:

The people you surround yourself with will have the biggest impact on you. Make sure you are surrounding yourself with those who can help you achieve your dreams.

Special Nugget for When Girls Win!

When Girls Win, we know that it takes a village to help us reach our truest potential and greatness. We don't go at it alone—we seek sage advice and counsel. Never be afraid to ask for advice and remember, we are all teachers...*and* students, too!

I JUST WANNA SHINE

Do what you can. Do what you have to do. Step outside of yourself. Be more. Be better. Be bigger than you've ever been before.

–Megan Rapinoe, Olympic Gold Medalist Team (USA women's soccer)

We had a top 4.0 biology major and Academic All-American on our team once who was also a talented golfer. She did not have a significant amount of junior golf tournament experience, but she had a lot of grit. Despite her natural gifts and determination, one critical issue kept holding her back—her perfectionist mindset. She was driven to be perfect—even though golf psychologist guru Bob Rotella advises us otherwise in his book, *Golf is Not a Game of Perfect.*

During her junior year, she made a commitment to see if she could loosen the grip of her perfectionism and adjust her mindset. She embraced every mental toughness tool and worked hard on becoming the mentally strongest player in the field.

Developing a champion mindset is like mastering any other skill. It takes consistent effort and commitment. It's paying attention to the small things and doing it over and over and over again. You wouldn't expect to pick up the trumpet and start marching in the band the next day. Do the reps, baby!

At one tournament in Monterey, our Academic All-American found herself just 3 strokes behind going into the final round. She was in the final group with the leaders and ready to go. She parred the first few holes but then had double bogeys on the 3rd and 4th holes, and quickly fell behind by 7 strokes with 14 holes left to play. I saw her second double bogey, and I must admit, I thought she was digging herself in deeper.

When I looked over at her across the green after she sank a three-foot putt to save the second double, she surprisingly smiled at me with a genuine smile. She walked over to get a water and her smile only got bigger. I was ready to give her an encouraging word or two, but instead the reverse happened when she said, "We've got this, Coach!" I quickly smiled back so not to show any concern, and said, "Okay, let's go!"

Then as she was walking over to pick up her bag, she enthusiastically waved over at her teammate across the fairway as she confidently moved on to the next tee box. I promptly checked live scoring because I thought maybe I had been wrong about her score. I knew she had hit one into a penalty area where she took a 1-stroke penalty and that she had missed her approach shot, but maybe I missed something? Yes, it was a double—two in a row in dark blue, which on Golfstat means over par. If I had not witnessed her misses, and seen it posted in dark blue, I would have thought for certain she had scored a birdie instead! Wow!

I was so impressed with her unshakeable attitude and mindset. I could feel her positive energy, so I took off to watch my other players.

By the time our Academic All-American got to the 12th hole, I instantly recognized the glazed-over look in her eyes. Yep—it was there. The zone had found her. I checked her scores and now, there were lots of red posts signaling that she was shooting under par!

At this point, I knew my job was to just cheer her on and watch from afar—it was quite a clinic she was putting on for her group and gallery. Three birdies in a row on the back 9 and six total since the 4th hole! One of them was on a hole that she had trouble with both in the practice round and the day before. This day, she striped it down the middle on the tight hole, hit a great approach to 10 feet and made a slippery side hill clutch putt. You go, girl!

By the 18th hole, she had sealed the deal with one last birdie! Our team won the tournament, and oh by the way, she did, too! Her mindset and her love for the team that day were indescribable. I wish I had taken a video of her performance because many would not believe her complete resilience and commitment to her positive attitude. She maintained a winning mindset from the minute she teed it up and never veered off it, no matter what challenges were thrown her way.

She told me afterwards that she set her positive vibe and then used her love for her teammates as her anchor to play to her potential that day. She had me in tears. Happy tears, of course. (Note: I am still crying as I type this—the Italian in me, and I can't help it—but it's a phenomenal feeling when your player finds it and lives it!). Watching a player completely surrender the outcome and perform at their highest level is surreal for a coach. You believe in your players, but never know if they can dig deep enough to get there. This player did—with confidence.

Mental Toughness Training Tip:

Your competitive advantage is your winning mindset and positive energy. Mentally tough people are not more talented—just more consistent. That is critical in getting to a higher level of play. You set an intention that you are going to stay in that state no matter what challenges the competition brings. You control what you can control: your mindset.

I believe this player summed up the ultimate answer that we all are searching for whenever we walk out onto our field of play. The winning mindset does *not* guarantee a trophy every time, but it does mean a win for your inner game. That's what we are striving for—*a peaceful inner spirit*—because that is where our magic lies.

UNSTOPPABLE

When we can walk away from our competition knowing that we allowed our innate ability to play, and we maintained harmony between our left brain (ego and controlling) and our right (let it happen) brain, we win no matter what the outcome shows. We trust our hard work and practice and believe we will do well. We stay free from focus on results and trying too hard. We relax, act like a winner the entire time, and bring a warrior spirit.

I have to admit, it's not an easy place to get to. Our negative bias and ego like to take over, especially after we make a mistake. It's a definite challenge not to let self-anger and doubt creep in. We have to prepare for the obstacles and be ready for anything. FEAR may stand for False Evidence Appearing Real, but when it's taking over it can *feel* so very real.

Courage is a big part of finding the magic. As James Taylor says in his song, *Secret of Life*, "It's okay to feel afraid, don't let it stand in your way." We need to embrace our fears and have more courage to let go of them. James continues, "The goal is to not try too hard," after all, "it's just a lovely ride."[1]

Do you have the courage to let go of your ego and bring joy out every time you tee it up or compete or just get out of bed for that matter? Can you always show up with a powerful and winning mindset? What if you hook it out of bounds on the 1st hole? Will you chalk it up to a bad day from the get-go, or be able to let go and not link that one errant shot with any other shot? It was a standalone nuisance. Just one.

The other key to this player's superior performance was her love, joy, and gratitude for the opportunity to play for the team. She never veered from those feelings, and it fueled her with unbelievable power and inner strength.

Mental Toughness Training Tip:

You have amazing power and music within you. It's not our ego talking, it's the gifts that we have been given. Recognize your gifts and be joyful and grateful that you get the opportunity to be in the arena.

"A legend is just an ordinary person with extraordinary determination!" This quote is often attributed to the American basketball player and coach, Coach Jimmy Valvano also known as Jimmy V.[2] Many others have said it in similar ways.

To become great, it doesn't matter who you are. If you don't get to play club sports, or you are not picked first, or you find yourself on the B Team, or you don't even get recruited, it's okay. You can still be great! Go after what you want and what you are passionate about. Passion drives everything. Many times, we want to settle or talk ourselves out of our greatness because it is hard work. We sabotage ourselves a lot of time because we compare too much, instead of finding our own gifts. We think it's already been taken.

I used to think that way myself on the putting green. If someone sunk a 40-footer, my 30-footer seemed impossible. I would think, *how can I make this now?* Instead of saying, "Awesome, now it's my turn."

It takes time to grow with your physical talents and your mental skills, but once you find that place, it's a feeling like no other. Let's go—you have the music in you!

"The meaning of life is to find your gift. The purpose is to share it!!" said the incomparable Pablo Picasso.

Special Nugget for When Girls Win!

When Girls Win, we understand that mental toughness involves believing in the greatness inside of us right down to our core. We all have inspiring music in us, but it takes consistency and finding and building the confidence so we can get there.

We know that the choice is ours--to look at obstacles as problems or as opportunities. We don't let the obstacles keep us from being our best selves. We make it more about what we have to give. We remember that everything is preparing us for the next level, and we truly embrace it with courage. We tap into our built-in bravery.

Remember this.

"The greatest danger for most of us is not that our aim is too high, and we miss it, but that it is too low, and we reach it." Michelangelo

YOU CAN DO MAGIC

Siri, Can you play 'We are the Champions?'

–Coach MaryJo McCloskey,
2023 NCAA D-III Women's Golf National Champion Coach

Yessssss!!! We did it! We reached the top of the mountain! We arrived at our destiny! Top of the Leaderboard! Top of the Podium! The journey is all about learning, but if you reach that auspicious destination that you have been chasing for quite some time, it's truly a dream come true. That dream came true for me and our amazing team just as I was finishing up this book. What timing—who knew that *this* would be the year?

How did our team do it? What was the difference? How did we beat some magnificent odds? Let's just say it was a culmination of hard work, passion, process and *all* the mental toughness work we've shared here. The stars aligned and it came together. The *magic* was all around us, and we embraced it and invited it into our play!

No, we did not try harder. No, we did not wear the same socks every day. No, we did not play the exact same tunes in the van or wear the same color scrunchies in our hair. We did stay with our confidence, belief, process, and a strategic plan for all four rounds. We showed up ready and believed we could do it, and we did!

On the final round, we struggled some on the front 9, and even though we had fallen slightly behind with 9 holes to play, our confidence and winning mindset never wavered. That is when our grit and resilience from all our training kicked in *big time*. We had the best back 9 of any other team shooting under par! Our senior (and captain) was on fire from the 9th hole on. It was a storybook finish and a total team effort!

Mental Toughness Training Tip:

Stay with your process. Always stay confident when you are in the arena. Never say never, and never ever give up!

HOW IT WENT DOWN

As we headed into the National Championship, I knew without a doubt our team was prepared. We had won our Conference Championship with three players shooting rounds under par and our team was beautifully pumped to get to the famed Howey-in-the-Hills, Florida—a place I had visited five times before with different teams to take the big stage at the National Championship.

Physically, we needed to quickly adjust to the Floridian heat and climate in addition to the three-hour East Coast time change. We also had to adapt to the challenging grain of Bermuda grass in terms of chipping and putting—a vast difference from the Poana grass in the Pacific Northwest that doesn't impact a player's short game as much.

Most importantly, we needed to be prepared mentally for the Championship—the Mission Inn course did not get nicknamed, "Mission Impossible" for no reason. We needed to create a mindset that could rise above having a potential bad hole or two or even three. We needed to realize that shooting 5 or 6 over par could still be a great score on such a challenging course. I taped four scorecards together to show the players exactly how many holes they'd be playing and demonstrating that getting upset over one bad shot or one bad hole would only be a waste of time in the bigger picture of 72 holes.

As teams started showing up for the first round, I was a little jealous (only for a minute) to see a couple nice Mercedes team vans pull in. I then spotted some top recruits from a nearby prestigious golf academy heading out to follow other teams and coaches but not us. We felt like underdogs, but it didn't matter.

Our team hopped out of our rental van and started preparing as we always do. Some nervous energy? Yes, but also some total excitement to have this opportunity to compete. We were having fun from the moment we arrived because we knew we were prepared. We'd done the work and the mental prep. We did our traditional arrival video for social media and that was our celebratory kick-off.

Mental Toughness Training Tip

Preparation is everything. Remember, you can't show up trying to find it. You must always arrive ready.

KNOW WHEN TO HOLD 'EM, KNOW WHEN TO FOLD 'EM

Day One finally arrived. Our first player teed off and pulled her drive into the trees down the left of the fairway. I won't take you through the entire hole, but let's just say it was not the type of first hole start she had visualized. Remember, surprises happen. She did not panic. She accepted and moved on. BAM! Her teammate playing behind her, never saw any negative behavior or body language to imply she had a difficult start. The putt she made could have been for a par. She seemed comfortable and focused. Exactly what we had talked about.

The 13th hole was a difficult hole and had a very tricky pin placement on Day One. One of our players who started brilliantly that day actually 4-putted it. After the round, the other coaches in my group and I mentioned it to the tournament committee and the rules officials that they needed to be careful where they put the pins during the week as it was already a challenging course, and the pins didn't need to exaggerate the difficulty of the greens even more. They told us they would be careful.

The greens at Mission Inn have a lot of undulation to them and having a downhill putt is almost impossible to stop. On some of the tougher greens, there were only two or three small sections of the green that were level enough for the pin placement. The problem was that many cups had been placed in those sections so that players would be required to putt over old cups. In order to avoid that, the rules officials seemed to be looking for other hole locations on the greens.

Round One was not our best round, but we stayed mentally focused and finished in second position behind the leader. As we warmed up for the second round, I overheard a spectator on the first tee ask someone where our university was located. Instead of Googling it on her phone, the other spectator mentioned that he thought we were from Georgia. Makes sense! No one could imagine that a university from the Pacific Northwest could possibly compete in the Southeast.

After finishing the very challenging *Gauntlet Holes* 4, 5 and 6 (as our school President named them), we had moved from 2nd to 7th on the scoreboard. Anyone watching the live action, saw our players remain relaxed, giving it their best on every shot. Our players did not show emotion. After a short thunderstorm delay, our team came back strong, and by the end of the day, we had climbed our way back up the leaderboard and found ourselves on top after two rounds—36 holes.

I was really happy for our team after the round and how hard they had worked on staying focused to move themselves back to the top. I think my excitement may have triggered one of the other coaches somehow who felt the need to tell me that his team had been in the same position another year, only to falter and not finish in one of the podium positions. Basically, he was reminding me that there was a lot of golf left and to not get too excited.

Obviously, I was very knowledgeable that the tournament was a long way from being over, but I believe it's important to always celebrate the small wins—and in that moment, we felt like we won the day.

Mental Toughness Training Tip

Celebrate your time in the arena and your small wins. Realize that there will be chatter and gamesmanship but always let it go. Control what you can control.

That evening my phone was going crazy as our families and supporters were so excited by our performance. We were demonstrating our strength and that we were good enough to go the distance. We had done our job so to speak. But the team knew they needed to continue the streak—they'd created such a bond and believed in our strategy so much; they were on a mission to be on top at the end of the fourth and final round. No getting ahead of ourselves. It was only half-time.

For the third round, we were paired with the other top two teams in the standings. The potential distractions of streaming TV and more spectators showing up didn't seem to faze our team. They continued to believe in themselves and fully owned their games.

KEEP ON TRUCKIN', BABY

Even though we had discussed a new strategy for tackling those gauntlet holes, we once again struggled through them. When we got to the 6th hole, the pin position was placed on a 5 percent slope, making it truly an unfair pin. I watched one of our players hit a great putt that rolled all the way off the green. It was a bad pin placement, but it didn't break our team's spirit. As some coaches were expressing their frustrations at rules officials who stood nearby, we continued with business, understanding they made a mistake and quietly moved on.

The gauntlet holes were having an impact on every team that day. For that reason, I was never so proud of our team. We never gave in to the negativity. We continued as we had during the previous days staying true to ourselves and our games. We had dropped a little off the leaderboard, but once again, had a big rally on the back 9 with one of our players making four birdies and another shooting 1 over for the entire day. We were back on top of the leaderboard with the top 12 seeded teams having all finished the third round.

However, later that afternoon, thunderstorms arrived, and play was suspended for those teams still playing in the afternoon rounds. During that time, the brutal pin placement on the 6th hole became a hot discussion item as a decision was made to water the 6th green at some point in the afternoon, thus, potentially making the putting less severe for some of the teams. What? Remember, 12 teams had already finished the course as-is and many other teams from the afternoon wave had finished that hole.

Since this was the cut day for teams (best 15 teams stay to play the final round and others are cut from the field), some teams were livid saying an advantage had been given after the watering occurred. Videos started popping up on social media of players putting on the 6th green, showing putts going up to the hole, slightly missing and then retreating back past the original point of origination.

Four schools, us being one of them, had separated ourselves from the field that day in terms of scoring, yet a campaign seemed to ensue about the unfairness of that pin position. Once the thunderstorms hit, and play could no longer continue that evening, no one knew what the schedule was going to be for the final day or how the cut was going to be done. Then a shocking email was sent out by the NCAA committee around 8pm that night saying the committee decided to completely *cancel* the third round including all 18 holes—even with a majority of teams having finished. Whatever campaign took place to make this happen, worked.

Unheard of! I couldn't believe it! How do you cancel a round in the middle of a tournament when all of the leading teams had completed the round and had finished playing that hole? Only a few teams who were way down the leaderboard had not yet played that hole. The committee announced that because the third round would be cancelled, they would make the cut to 15 teams based on the second round and go back to the second-round results to start the final round. So instead of allowing the third round to finish the next day in the morning—which is usually what happens after an afternoon thunderstorm delay and no daylight is left to go back out—the committee decided to cancel the round, make the cut, and move on.

Over 60 percent of the field had finished the third round, yet cancelling those scores based on that one poor pin placement ended up being the decision. I was in shock. This has never happened in NCAA history before where a mid-round was completely canceled. Final rounds have been canceled but not mid-rounds.

Our team had just played their hearts out. We had a player who had climbed the individual leaderboard from 10th place and who was in 2nd place and could very likely be the leader going into the final round. Several players and teams fought hard that day on the course and moved above the cut line as well, and it all meant nothing—and those who didn't play well that day received a huge gift with this decision. It seemed like those who screamed the loudest were heard. I even heard that the rules official on the 6th hole had to leave because of all the negativity being expressed.

I called the Committee Chair that evening to ask for an appeal, as I am a big believer in the golf course deciding the results—not a committee. But he wasn't sure of the appeal process.

Did they understand they were *canceling* players' scores? He informed me that the USGA provided the committee with options, and they picked this one. When I asked what the other options were, I was told that I should just trust the committee. Of course, at that point, social media was blowing up as word got out before I even had a chance to tell our players. All the scores from the day were quickly erased from Golfstat as well. I knew the committee was trying their best, but I still didn't agree with the decision.

I was not happy. I could not understand why they simply did not just cancel that one hole for everyone across the board if necessary. After-all, we had played 18 holes and don't those other 17 holes matter?

Then I remembered a quote I had recently heard, "Anger only weakens you." I could not be angry. Was it fair? No. Was it the right decision? No, not in my opinion. But it is what happened and just like on the course, you have to accept uncontrollable challenges and move on.

Yikes—this one would be a challenge for me emotionally, but I had to let go, find my peaceful place, and then rally our team. Remember resilience, grit, and determination—and staying the course, so to speak? This called for a heavy dose of it!

I ran upstairs at the resort to meet with our players. I was a little worried about their mood and if I could lift them back up. They had truly given it their all that day and their performance didn't deserve to be cancelled. I also knew that teams that received a reprieve from their disappointing rounds would be reenergized.

The entire team was surprised by the decision, but their complete calmness in that moment inspired me. They said it didn't seem fair, but that they were ready for any and all adversity, and they would just head back out and get it done the next day. No problem. Even our player who had been on the top of the leaderboard cheered everyone on and said, "Let's go, we can do it, team!"

YOU AIN'T SEEN NOTHIN' YET!

The morning of the final round, our players all arrived smiling and ready to go. We went through our van routine, played some pump-up music, and went over some strategy reminders. I felt comfortable knowing we had done all that we could to be ready for this moment.

Plus, the team embodied great energy, high spirits, and positive attitudes—and that's all you can ask for as a coach!

After four holes or so, we were slowly losing the 5-shot lead we had started with. I had decided that I wasn't going to change what we had been doing. We had already discussed our plan. I would be there if I saw one of our players in trouble, if a player waved me over or if I needed to remind the players to eat or drink. However, I wasn't going to interrupt them if they were in the flow. I also steered clear of looking at results and didn't check the live scoring until we started the back 9 and we were tied for the lead.

Whoa. This was a test for me. Do I trust our team strategy just as we did the previous three days? Did I need to get more involved? I told myself to stay back. I had to allow the players to trust their instincts and play. It was hard to be a cheerleader and not be more involved. I knew it was more important to maintain faith in our team and our hard work, even though fear was creeping in on me as we moved closer to finishing.

Mental Toughness Training Tip

You must trust the mental work you've done—the mindset training you know sustains you. When the interference hits and doubt creeps in, let it go, relax, breathe, and allow the zone to find you.

On the 13th hole, I watched our senior from 140 yards out, knock in her second shot for an eagle on a difficult uphill par 4 hole. I knew right then that *magic* had hit. This was our programs 13th time at the National Championship, and it may be an unlucky number for some, but it was not going to be for us. When her shot went in, I had a feeling we were going to reach the top of our mountain.

I knew the magic was happening, but could we keep it? The hard part at this stage is getting through the tremendous amount of interference, both from inside and on the outside. Could we stay relaxed, and could all our mental toughness training get us to the finish line?

I was concerned by the huge scoreboard on the 15th tee box, as it was hard to miss. I knew all our players would have a hard time avoiding it. In the end, the scoreboard worked in our favor and fired up our team, as we went on to have four more birdies after that hole.

Our preparation had paid off. Our hard work paid off. It was a true all-around team effort and the trust I had in my players—and that they had in themselves—helped us get it done! After earning 13 visits to the Natties, we were the NCAA D-III National Champions, winning by the 5-stroke lead we had started with.

GIMME SOME LOVIN'

The biggest message I want to scream from the rooftops is that *the magic* is in all of us! Your *greatness* resides inside you. Release all the questioning and doubting. Keep working hard and having fun with the sport—or job or craft—you are passionate about. Greatness will be there for you, but only if you allow it to be. Even if it just comes in small spurts, it is in you. Negativity and fear love to squash our greatness—and we end up getting in our own way.

Anyone can achieve great things if they set their mind to it. We were not the favorite this year. We were not voted the #1 team at any point during the year. Many thought we were over-ranked being in the top 5 nationally. We didn't care. We knew we had put in the work and that we were capable of performing well.

In the end, hard work and mental toughness proved keys to becoming National Champions! Our team had finally conquered Howey—the El Campeon course at Mission Inn! This time, there was no fear, no crazy golf cart chases or personal comparisons involved. We had the music in us, and we played to our own fiercely authentic beat as we stayed resilient and won our inner games. We did not do it with a perfect performance but with a *believing* one—right down to our hearts and souls!

Special Nugget for When Girls Win!

When Girls Win, we know that anger will only weaken us in our battles. We find a way to achieve a higher vibe so we can remain calm and always ready to climb higher. We know greatness is within us.

We also know that sometimes you can have a lead and lose it and that's okay, too. Competition can come down to a few inches, a few putts, or a few strokes. If you keep getting back up, keep learning, keep growing, keep paying attention to the great music inside of you, you will go on to achieve great things. Let's go!

Photo Courtesy George Fox University

PERSPECTIVE

"Play big—and play for something bigger than yourself. You have a platform to be a role model for other people." Those are the words 2023 US Open champion Wyndham Clark heard from his mom just before she passed away from cancer when he was in college.[1]

Our team rose to a higher level when we started making our own commitment to a higher purpose and a greater calling. One nonprofit organization we find incredibly motivational is the Folds of Honor foundation (FOH), which provides life-changing educational scholarships to the spouses and children of America's fallen heroes and disabled military.

The FOH tribute program was created by the Women's Golf Coaches Association (WGCA) and Golf Coaches Association of America (GCAA) and offers an opportunity for any collegiate golf program to honor a fallen or severely wounded American service member. During play, team members take turns carrying a golf bag displaying the name, rank, and branch of service of the soldier or service member being honored.

Our team carried a golf bag honoring Second Lieutenant Mark Jennings Daily—he was my dear friend and college roommate's son. Second Lt. Mark was in the U.S. Army and paid the ultimate sacrifice in 2007 when he was killed in Iraq by an improvised explosive device. He was 23. He was a new husband. He had so much more life to live.

This man was all about serving others and doing his part to fight for freedom. He had dedicated his short life to that mission. His picture and his story were clipped to the side of the golf bag we dedicated in his honor—and each team member took turns carrying the special remembrance from one golf event to the next.

Not only was Second Lt. Mark's courageous story an inspiration to all of us, but it gave us incredible context on what's truly important. His memory became—and still is—a major influence on our team. Indeed, playing for something greater than ourselves put our games in true perspective—how can a missed putt or a mistake or even a loss mean anything when you have this kind of life-or-death reminder?

The challenges we face in the sports arena are just part of a game but as our journey continued, a deeper sense of gratitude for all who have served and given of themselves became an important motivational part of our program.

As our team started concentrating on perspective and gratitude, magic started happening. The game was no longer just about *us* but about a *bigger picture*. While the game of golf hasn't necessarily allowed us to 'serve others,' we all feel a much deeper appreciation for the opportunity we've been given to use our gifts. We came to see that others are not always afforded that same liberty. We also make sure we give back to our community each year as a team because we do believe our ultimate mission—to serve others.

I invite you to walk tall with gratitude, faith, perspective, and love—in any pursuit. It is there you will find your own magic.

SPECIAL NOTE

Music plays a *major* role on our journey as *music is magic!*

The chapters titles are all based on songs. Here are the chapter titles and the artists!

1. *I've Got the Music in Me* – Kiki Dee & The Kiki Dee Band
2. *Will it Go Round in Circles* – Billy Preston
3. *Turn the Beat Around* – Vicki Sue Robinson
4. *Rock the Boat, Baby!* – The Hues Corporation
5. *Don't Stop Me Now* – Queen
6. *Good Vibrations* – The Beach Boys
7. *Gonna' Fly Now* – Bill Conti (Rocky)
8. *Walking on Sunshine* – Katrina and the Waves
9. *Pick up the Pieces* – Average White Band
10. *Super Trouper* – ABBA
11. *Tell me Something Good* – Ewan McVicar
12. *Eye of the Storm* – Ryan Stevenson
13. *You Get What You Give* – New Radicals
14. *Under Pressure* – Queen
15. *Love Yourself* – Justin Bieber

16. *Ain't No Mountain High Enough* – Marvin Gaye & Tammi Terrell
17. *I've Got to use My Imagination* – Gladys Knight & the Pips
18. *Blank Space* – Taylor Swift
19. *I Will Survive* – Gloria Gaynor
20. *Not All Heroes Wear Capes* – Adam Young
21. *I Just Wanna Shine* – Fitz and The Tantrums
22. *You Can do Magic* – America

There are also other song titles sprinkled throughout the book! Here are those subtitles and artists:

We Came to Play – Tower of Power
Sweet Emotion – Aerosmith
Emotional Rescue – Rolling Stones
Go Where You Wanna Go – The Mamas & the Papas
Start Me Up – The Rolling Stones
Got Me Under Pressure – ZZ Top
One Love – Bob Marley
Build Me Up Buttercup – The Foundations
Stop, Look, Listen To Your Heart – The Stylistics
Can't Stop the Feeling! – Justin Timberlake
Up on a Tight Rope – Leon Russell
Work to Do – Average White Band
Ain't No Stoppin' us Now – McFadden & Whitehead
Something Big – Tom Petty
Higher Love – Steve Winwood
I Won't Back Down – Tom Petty
Get Up Stand Up – Bob Marley
Dream On – Aerosmith
Suddenly I See – KT Tunstall
Blame it on the Boogie – The Jackson 5
Let it Go – Idina Menzel
Just Breathe – Faith Hill
Ride Like the Wind – Christopher Cross

You've Got a Friend – James Taylor
Got To Be Real – Cheryl Lynn
Help I need Somebody – The Beatles
Unstoppable – Sia
Know when to hold 'em, know when to Fold 'em – Kenny Rogers
Keep on Truckin' – Eddie Kendricks
You Ain't Seen Nothin' Yet – Bachman–Turner Overdrive
Gimme Some Lovin' – The Spencer Davis Group

Cheers to finding YOUR own *authentic* beat!

Coach MJ

APPENDIX 1: MENTAL TOUGHNESS TRAINING TIPS SUMMARY

CHAPTER 1

1. Mistakes and setbacks are what taught me to succeed. I have learned my greatest lessons from defeat. Those lessons can be extremely tough and make you want to run the other way— but persevering through the challenges provides the lessons and strength to get to a higher level. Failures are actually necessary in order to grow and understand how to succeed.

2. If you think you have less of an advantage because you are a girl, you <u>will have</u> less of an advantage because you are one. I never once thought that our women's teams had any less of an advantage. Plus, if you think you are not good enough, you will not be good enough. I never once thought that our team would not be good enough.

3. Passion plays a huge role in achieving success. If you have a driving passion to accomplish something, you will work harder and you will achieve more! It's important to "get in the car!" Get onboard! There is a road to success—but it's not a

straight one to the finish line. It will be winding, bumpy and uphill a lot of times, but it's there for you to drive.

4. Talent is not everything. Energy and mental toughness often surpass talent and experience!

5. Face the obstacles, observe your resistance, and you will be on your way to achieving success in whatever you undertake!

CHAPTER 2

1. Motivation should always be stated in the POSITIVE! Abandon trying **not** to do something. The brain does not recognize the negative. You have probably heard the famous saying, "If you try **not** to think of a pink elephant, what comes to your mind?" Exactly: A pink elephant! I was always trying not to lose, and guess what happened? Yes, I lost. I should have been trying to WIN.

2. Remember that greatness is born from losing and failing. Every elite athlete suffers losses but learns from failure. Those lessons boost them to higher levels of achievement. Losing teaches resilience and makes you stronger for the next time— as long as you learn and grow from your setbacks.

3. Becoming more self-aware of your actions and reactions in competitive situations is super critical for growth and success! It always starts and ends with YOU. Accepting responsibility is crucial to taking your game to another level. Blame will not help.

4. Speeding around in circles is a good analogy for what can happen when emotions win the day. Emotional negativity has a physiological effect that clouds your thinking and decision-making ability. Plus, if your competitor sees you are upset, emotional, weak, and driven by ego, game over!

5. Becoming mentally tough takes practice to create winning mental strength. Use imagery and visualization, journaling, meditating, breathing exercises, and affirmations to advance

your game—on the course and in life. This sounds easy, but hard to do. Remember, practice is key.

CHAPTER 3

1. How you feel inside will reflect on the outside. When you react, you give away your power. When you stay emotionally resilient, you set up for success.
2. Focus on what you want. State things with intention rather than what you are trying to avoid. Always be committed to the outcome you want.
3. Radiating positive energy is one of the best ways to stay emotionally grounded. As your confidence escalates, you find yourself in the winners' circle more often. Growing stronger mentally takes time—consistently observing yourself and understanding what makes you tick and what triggers you are keys to competing and winning in any arena.

CHAPTER 4

1. ALWAYS dream big! We all have callings but most of the time, we squash them down with excuses. If you are passionate and you want something, keep that energy, and go after it. Even if you fall short, you will have no regrets and will achieve much more than if you didn't try at all!
2. Learn all you can from the best around you. Never think or assume you know it all—as that is ego-driven and will not improve your standing! Embrace a mastery mindset—learning and improving is important if you want to keep growing and advancing to another level. The rewards will eventually find you.
3. Success is in the details. Always pay attention to the details in everything you do. They can make a world of difference in elevating mood and a winning attitude. They can also be the

difference in one or two strokes on the golf course (paying close attention to wind shifts on a golf course, low points of a putting green, etc.). Details rule.

4. Let go of expectations! You can expect to perform well but know that situations arise that you cannot control. You can never control how anyone else acts or performs. Shine your own light. Focus on YOUR greatness. And above all, keep the big picture in mind.

5. You cannot control what others think of you. Stay on your path with a positive mission in mind. When someone vents something intentionally hurtful, shake it off and remember that YOU are meant to be there to do powerful, transformative work. Show up, endeavor to grow, and voice your ideas. You possess greatness and were born to shine.

CHAPTER 5

1. You will face uncomfortable situations in sports, business, or at various times in your life no matter what. Understanding and learning how to accept them and staying within your own zone will only make you stronger and likely lead to the best outcome.

2. Believe in your goals and own your own game. It might feel cool to be accepted by your peers, but is that worth sacrificing your ultimate pursuit? Putting in only half the work, energy, effort, and commitment will not advance you to your goal. Your personal journey and the why of what you're doing are key to your success. Why do you get up in the morning? Why do you pursue your sport? In the end, your persistence—and honoring your passion—are what will help you fly higher and farther.

3. Running from negative emotions will only give them more strength and divert you from your mission. The key is to know why your passion drives you, so negative emotions will not

sway you from your goal. You hone your inner game and commitment to rise above the fear of not being good enough or fitting in.

4. Understand—and release—what you can't control. Period. So many things are out of your control: the weather, what others think of you, your pairings and playing partners, the wind, course conditions, and pin placements. You name it. Focus on what you can control—your attitude, your mindset, and especially your belief in yourself!

5. Always remember that your adversaries are your best teachers. Big lesson here. You can get angry, mad, upset, frustrated, whatever, but they can teach you more than you ever imagined. Pay attention to what your rivals are teaching you. There's no mistake they are on your path for a reason. Be aware. Learn the lessons—and use them to your advantage. Trust me, you'll grow immensely and emerge victorious.

6. Shrugging off what others think of you is so important to personal growth and building confidence. No one knows what you may be going through. Always focus on your own goals and never let peer pressure and judgment impact your journey.

CHAPTER 6

1. From 1 to 10 (1 being relaxed and 10 being tense) what is your ideal energy level when you are performing at your best? Once you know your ideal performance number, you can adjust with tactics for when you're feeling too low or too intense. To inspire yourself, have a motivational phrase or song in mind even if you have to sing the anthem to yourself! If you're amped or anxious, deep focused breathing is the best technique to slow your roll. Getting to your optimum rhythm enables you to compete at higher levels more consistently.

2. Be sure to have personal mantra or inspirational tune to help you ramp up your winning energy. If you're in over-drive, remember deep breathing will slow your heart rate and ease you back to your zone. Breath is a dynamic power source. If you are feeling anxious, with just a few deep breaths, you can help to maintain the best cortisol level for performance. The 4-7-8 breathing method seems to be one of the best methods used for athletes. Inhale to the count of 4, hold for 7 seconds and then exhale for 8. Give it a go—it works!

3. Self-awareness of your optimal energy level is critical to performing at your best. Understanding your own needs, what inspires you and how to return to your best optimal energy state are key to improving and winning. We are all motivated differently, learn differently, and have different levels of excitement and energy. There is no one-size-fits-all solution.

CHAPTER 7

1. It's critical to stay patient with the process and know that building the blocks of consistency wins. It's not a sprint but a continual marathon to growth and improvement.

2. Set a goal and visualize yourself achieving it. Critical!

3. Patience is a superpower for success. Allow yourself time to get to your destiny!

4. The journey is about patience and persistence. Stay on the marathon journey to greatness. It's in you. Many give up before the magic truly sparks. Know it's there and keep advancing. One percent better each day does add up to that winning percentage eventually.

5. Act like a champion before you are champion. You can't be a champion until you see yourself being a champion.

6. Work on getting one percent better each day. We may not always feel like doing the work but being consistent each day brings bigger improvement and success.

CHAPTER 8

1. Winning comes from finding your way to the highest vibration which is joy! Joy in your hard work. Joy in your progress. Joy in striving toward a bigger goal. Joy in the special moments along the way. Joy in the opportunity to play or coach a sport that you love! The winning is in the joy. It's the gift for getting to do what you love and the freedom to be in a state where fear does not exist. It does not mean you'll always earn a trophy, but if you continue in a high vibe mindset—success will find you.

2. Understand that we all have emotions, but if you can learn to observe the negative ones and continue to focus on joy and doing what you love, you will find more positivity and success. Plus, you will create a stronger edge over the competition.

CHAPTER 9

1. A reminder to DREAM BIG! Make your goal to WIN. Never to just show up.

2. Preparation is everything. Be prepared for all the challenges you will face. Have a plan before arriving at your competition takes diligence but will help you feel ready when you get there and separate you from the competition. The more you can see yourself in the moment before you are actually in it, the better prepared you will be.

3. In tension-filled situations, use your senses as much as possible to stay in the now. It may sound strange, but it works. Focusing on your feet on the ground or the smells in the air or the breeze on your cheeks keeps you away from worry and anxiety about the future outcome or past mistakes you made.

4. Mental toughness training is an ongoing process. Many times, we must go back to our toolbox for help find what works best for us.

5. Your routine keeps you in the moment and works as your safety net. It is calming to your mind to do it the same way each time and reduces anxiety and stress. Lock into your successful routines whether you are a coach or a player. Also remember besides looking like you belong, FEEL like you belong. You have earned it.

6. You do you! PERIOD! Trust your own game. If you have one eye on someone else's game, how can you truly focus on your own? TRUST YOURSELF. Be YOU. It's **you versus you** out there and no one else.

7. As you get to a higher level and the competition becomes even more fierce, your mental toughness training and commitment must continue to get stronger. You have to learn to block out what others are doing; and understand that your competitors are going to play great as well. You must learn to ride their momentum and view it positively like "If they play well, I can too." This more positive outlook keeps your emotions intact. Basically, the goal is always to focus on what you can control— YOU and YOUR MINDSET. No comparing yourself or your game with anyone else—or you will get distracted and end up in worse shape.

8. Reminder, elite competitors know what they can control and let go of the things they can NOT control.

9. Consistency wins. Leave overnight success to Fed Ex. Keep learning and growing each and every day. One percent improvement each day is better than trying for five percent on one day and zero the next. Trying to go for too much at once can wear you down over time. Consistency brings results. As Zen Monk, Shunryu Suzuki said, "In the beginner's mind, there are many possibilities, but in the expert's mind, there are few." cite) Always stay OPEN to the possibilities.

CHAPTER 10

1. Growth happens when you step outside your comfort zone. Many athletes know this but forget to practice it regularly or resist it because it's too uncomfortable. Learning to be comfortable when you are uncomfortable will help you grow and master the game.
2. Figuring out a way to get comfortable when you are in an uncomfortable situation is extremely important. If you resist and try to avoid the uncomfortable, your progress will remain limited.
3. Work on your weaknesses and find ways to hone those areas. If you avoid certain areas of your game, undoubtedly, you will face them in competition. Own them! The true magic lies outside your comfort zone.

CHAPTER 11

1. The key to more positive outcomes lies in your self-talk AND the stories you are telling yourself!! The more positive your thoughts, the more self-belief will inhabit your subconscious mind.
2. Writing positive affirmations and/or journaling about your successes and intentions will help invigorate your brain just like lifting weights strengthens your body.
3. The voice in your head can either help you win or help you lose. You get to choose. Focus on a positive voice and talk to yourself like you would talk to a teammate or friend. Be affirmative and anticipate positive outcomes.
4. Be your loudest cheerleader. Realize it's the negative self-talk that creates tension, stress, and defeat. Commit to positivity and confident self-talk and you will see an immediate difference in your performance.

CHAPTER 12

1. Figure out ways to get to yes by being tactical and smart. Understand all the facts and be willing to make the case that's best for all even if the loudest voices believe differently.
2. Do what you believe is right! You are not always going to win, but always stand up for what you think is right. Fortitude is powerful.
3. Create that steel bubble around you and fill it with mantras that keep you in a super confident, powerful place and enjoy the challenge. The strength you gain during adversity is unsurpassable.

CHAPTER 13

1. Focus on your daily process goals and the results will take care of themselves.
2. You can't control results, but you CAN control your process. Remember to celebrate the little victories as you pursue the bigger picture. Learn how to be process-oriented, and you will become much stronger in your sport.

CHAPTER 14

1. Pressure is your friend and fear is a liar. When pressure arrives, observe it, embrace it, honor it and you will break its stronghold. When you break through the resistance, you're on your way to the next level!
2. Trust all your hard work and your preparation. Let go of the false stories.
3. Pressure can make you feel like you are going to choke your guts out, but that's why the best athletes embrace the

discomfort and accept the situation. They know that in doing so, they can persevere and achieve so much more.

4. Be aware of tension in your body, feel it, and do a body scan before you compete. Breathe into any tense areas, visualize healing light, and observe the tension leaving your body. Experiencing yourself letting go of that tension is one of the best things you can do before a performance.

CHAPTER 15

1. Master your mindset and attitude. Reminder to release things you cannot control. The more you detach from all the things that are out of your control, the more you can focus on what you can guide—your mind and your attitude!

2. CHANGING your negative body language is one of the fastest ways to adjust your pessimistic vibe and arrive in a more positive state or flow. Simply adjusting your posture, standing tall and walking with confidence signals your mind that you've located your inner power and are in rhythm. It works and is quickly effective.

3. Ask yourself, in the heat of battle, do you want an enemy speaking to you or an ally? Of course, you want an ally, a trusted friend saying nice things to you and cheering you on. Change the tone in your head, be kinder to yourself and embrace the magic.

CHAPTER 16

1. Getting to the top of the podium is not just about recruiting talent; it's about recruiting passion and grit! Players need to be willing to do what needs to be done when the pressure is on. To be successful, you must commit to being all in and to playing with fortitude and tenacity.

2. It's important to be who you are and not let what others might think of you sway you off course. Others can help guide you, but success comes from within you.

3. Arriving in the arena is a challenge but staying there is even harder. Grit and courage are required especially during challenges. It's not always going to feel good. Keep the bigger picture in mind and listen to your heart.

CHAPTER 17

1. There is always a way around resistance. Remember the Navy Seal 40 percent rule? Even when you feel like quitting, just know you are closer to a breakthrough than you think. Winners breathe, learn, let go and keep going.

2. Take responsibility. Take responsibility for your mistakes. Take responsibility for the attitude you bring to your game. Take responsibility for how you treat your teammates and your coach. Take responsibility for your success with gratefulness and humility. Lose the ego-soaked excuses and you will excel much further in your sport and in life.

3. Reminder again: Accept and take responsibility for mistakes. You MUST be stronger mentally than your strongest excuse.

CHAPTER 18

1. Visualization and trust are vital components to staying in the moment and succeeding with the task at hand.

2. Once you feel confidence in your physical training, then rehearse letting it happen. Don't think, just do! Like the line in Caddyshack: "Be the ball."

3. Trust more and do less. Sometimes in more competitive situations we think we need to do more, be more, when we just need to trust more and be more accepting. That is true inner toughness right there.

4. No judging yourself while you are competing! The only focus should be staying with your process and watching the progress happen.
5. Letting it happen subconsciously means that you are executing your task with a clear, focused and trusting mindset. The more trust and belief you have in yourself, the more you will be free from control of the conscious mind.

CHAPTER 19

1. Embrace the pressure! Accept nerves and remind yourself that excitement is good. Nerves mean you are ready.
2. Think about potential surprises before your competition and visualize yourself handling them with a calm and confident attitude.
3. Showing up in the arena is a big part of growth. Surprises will happen, and how we deal with them is the real test. Laughing after you fought through them is pure joy.
4. Giving your best is knowing that you did everything you could. Having no regrets is fine as long as you learned from the experience. Celebrate the small wins as that will help motivate your subconscious mind in the future.

CHAPTER 20

1. Remember the great Zen master, Shunryu Suzuki quote, "In the beginner's mind, there are many possibilities, but an expert's, there are few." Always be open-minded, study those who excel and are at the top in your field and look for ways to improve and grow.
2. Build your power circle with people who will be truthful and tell you what you need to hear in order to improve. These are not people who always tell you what you want to hear–rather, people you trust to guide and inspire you. If you only listen to

your family or a few close friends, you are likely just scratching the surface of knowledge that is available to you.

3. Release ego and a need to control. Realize all the resources are available to you. The know-it-alls lose! Find honest advisors or books that can help you with your answers and needs. Ask questions. Seek mentors. Learn and grow from them. That's the name of the game.

4. The people you surround yourself with will have the biggest impact on you. Make sure you are surrounding yourself with those who can help you achieve your dreams.

CHAPTER 21

1. Your competitive advantage IS your winning mindset and positive energy. Mentally tough people are not more talented —just more consistent. That is critical in getting to a higher level of play. You set an intention that you are going to stay in that state no matter what challenges the competition brings. You control what you can control: your mindset.

2. You have amazing power and music within you. It's not our ego talking, it's the gifts that we have been given. Recognize your gifts and be joyful and grateful that you get the opportunity to be in the arena.

CHAPTER 22

1. Stay with your process. Always stay confident when you are in the arena. Never say never, and never ever give up!

2. Preparation is everything. Remember, you can't show up trying to find it. You must always arrive ready.

3. Celebrate your time in the arena and your small wins. Realize that there will be chatter and gamesmanship but always let it go. Control what you can control.

4. You must trust the mental work you've done—the mindset training you know sustains you. When the interference hits and doubt creeps in, let it go, relax, breathe, and allow the zone to find YOU.

APPENDIX 2: SPECIAL NUGGETS FOR WHEN GIRLS WIN

#1

We learn how to bring out our best selves by understanding the energy and vibe it takes to discover the great music that resides within. We believe the impossible is possible and our passion leads the way in helping us maneuver around the obstacles and break through the resistance.

#2

We use our emotions to our *advantage*. It's important that we remember to breathe to lower our cortisol level so we can find our neutral place and return there when we feel negative vibes creeping in. Tipping your emotional hand gives away your power. Envisioning yourself staying calm and relaxed in the face of fear and failure is key to maintaining your power. Emotional resilience keeps cortisol levels down, so we can think clearly and fly higher than we ever thought possible.

#3:

We continue to practice our emotional resilience when dealing with the small dramas in our lives, so we can be ready for the bigger stuff. It's easy to place blame on others, make excuses for our mistakes, and grouse about conditions. If we stay strong in our beliefs, focus on our intentions, and know that emotional resilience is our superpower in the most difficult situations, we have already won!

#4:

We are unapologetic about who we are and unafraid to stand tall, rock the boat when we need to, and radiate. Women have been in supporting roles for a very long time and finally understand that it's okay to be bold, to pursue our passion, and be a competitor in the arena. It's okay to embody strength, passion, and finish as a winner. Be courageous and success is yours!

#5:

We are focused on our own goals and worry-free about what others think. We release our people-pleasing insecurities and needs, so we can pursue and achieve our dreams, goals, and wins. With a deep-seeded belief in ourselves and our mission, we know that our dreams are possible and in time, we arrive to shine our inner greatness.

We also understand that we can channel negative emotions, like anger or frustration, into intense positive fuel to help us accomplish our mission. We achieve a higher level of success as we become true to our authentic and true selves—and less to ego. We own our game, our journey, our power, and ultimately, the greatness that we all have within us. This is not about arrogance—but using our gifts and talents to continue to climb to new heights.

#6:

We know that self-awareness is key to our success. We know how to get to our personal zone to perform at our highest level. We also know that maintaining our best personal energy level is key to our success.

#7:

We know that team *culture, chemistry* and *patience* are critical to success. Mutual support and encouragement are also part of the winning formula. We avoid the rush to get there and understand that slow and steady always wins the race!

#8:

We no longer seek ways to prove ourselves to anyone. We are true to ourselves and find joy following our passion. When we struggle with negative emotions, we know how to quickly get back to a higher vibration. We know that higher vibrational energy—Joy! —guarantees our best outcome.

With increased self-awareness, we learn to let go of things we can't control and stay in our own joyful place. We navigate roadblocks—even the political ones—and realize our power is founded in our joy and passion for the game.

#9:

We believe in ourselves to the fullest. We are free of fear and doubt, and we own who we are and what we have worked hard to achieve. Our confidence shines as we go after our goals knowing we are ready. We believe in who we are and our gifts and intelligence. Even in big moments, we remember to be ourselves and no one else!

#10:

We move outside our Comfort Zone to explore our potential and achieve more. We rehearse for any number of unforeseen scenarios on the course.

Finding that Magic Zone is critical to our success. Period. In any walk of life. Sure, that means more challenges and failures will inevitably occur–that's all part of the fun!

#11:

We stop beating ourselves up with our words. Negative thoughts will still arise, but our mental strength will help us respond more effectively and positively. We are kinder to ourselves and speak to ourselves and to others with much more grace and empathy. We have self-compassion and are gentler on ourselves for mistakes we make. Most importantly we forgive ourselves and choose a higher vibration like gratitude, joy, and love to progress. We know that mistakes will occur, and they are there to help us learn and improve.

#12:

We are more courageous, dauntless, and gutsy than we are given credit for. We know we are meant for greatness—and we press on. We never let anyone rain on our parade!

#13:

While we are striving for incredible results, we need to be in the moment. When our mind says, "think ahead about the score and how you want to finish," we lose the power of the moment and our process. Show up, do the work, and trust your process. Really. It's the only way to shine and achieve the results you want!

#14:

As Billie Jean King says, "Pressure is a privilege." We make pressure and fear our friends. We embrace pressure and honor fear knowing they are preparing us to get to advance, excel. The pressure of competition is a gift enabling us to further channel our greatness.

#15:

We are less critical of ourselves. We stop comparing and judging. We live in the moment and for the moments. We are grateful and joyful. We exude confidence, positive body language and always walk with pep in our step, head held high.

True Confidence comes from loving yourself!

#16:

We know that intimidating tactics will be used against us, but we keep our heads down, avoid emotion so we can think clearly, and persevere. Worrying about what others think will not get the job done or help you succeed. Stay true to your values and if others think less of you, know that is their problem, not yours.

As women coaches, we also know that in a male-dominated sport like golf, we will have difficulty earning status and respect. When Girls Win, we compete anyway and know we deserve to be there. We embody grit and courage and stay true to ourselves and our passion. We strive for excellence, take on the challenges in a positive way and understand that some people will judge us when we speak the truth.

#17:

We take responsibility for our actions, learn from them, and understand more about how powerful we truly are. Taking responsibility is freedom from trying to hide our downfalls. We see through the excuses and witness our strength when we own our behavior and the mistakes we have made.

We find creative solutions. As Marie Forleo says in her book titled, *Everything is Figureaoutable,* "The power isn't out there, it's in you."[5] We dive deeper and find unique ways around the blockades. Giving in is not an option. We trust our own inner wisdom and hear the guidance speak to us. We rely on our own strength and trust in our good energy.

#18:

We understand that we can overthink things and try too hard. We free ourselves from focusing on perfection and do the best we can. We worry less about ideal results and just try to win each moment/day with grateful hearts and trust.

#19:

We are ready for surprises because we know that being able to shift gears quickly is important both on and off the course. We celebrate our wins—no matter what—and keep marching on as we know more wins are in our future!

#20:

We know that it takes a village to help us reach our truest potential and greatness. We don't go at it alone—we seek sage advice and counsel. Never be afraid to ask for advice and remember, we are all teachers... *and* students, too!

#21:

We understand that mental toughness really involves believing in the greatness inside of us right down to your core. We all have inspiring music in us, but it takes consistency and finding and building the confidence, so we can get there.

We know that the choice is ours--to look at obstacles as problems or as opportunities. We don't let the obstacles keep us from being our best selves. We make it more about what we have to give. We remember that everything is preparing us for the next level, and we truly embrace it with courage. We tap into our built-in bravery.

Remember this.

"The greatest danger for most of us is not that our aim is too high, and we miss it, but that it is too low, and we reach it." Michelangelo

#22:

We know that anger will only weaken us in our battles. We find a way to achieve a higher vibe so we can remain calm and always ready to climb higher. We know greatness is within us.

We also know that sometimes you can have a lead and lose it and that's okay, too. Competition can come down to a few inches, a few putts, or a few strokes. If you keep getting back up, keep learning, keep growing, keep paying attention to the great music inside of you, you will go on to achieve great things. Let's go!

ACKNOWLEDGMENTS

I'm incredibly grateful for so many:

My amazing husband Rick, who is our team's "Equipment Manager." Thank you for everything you do for all of us. You are our true superpower!

My fantastic editor Claudia (CJ) Johnson. Thank you for your extraordinary work in helping my words pop off the page. You are brilliant in every way. Thank you for believing in me and all your incredible insights and support. I have learned so much from you and am forever grateful.

My wonderful technical editor and my sister Terri Wallo Strauss. Your attention to details and excellent writing skills are so appreciated. I would have many more exclamations points if it wasn't for you!

My two brothers: Edward and Steve. Your support and love mean the world to me. Steve, thanks for getting me in the business in the first place and for your trust and belief in me. Edward, thanks for all the analysis to help us win the Championship.

Debra (DT) Phillips, Cathie Shelton, Julie Johnson, Cindy McInnis, Debbi Maggio and Ingrid Pentecost who have spent countless hours listening to me over the years. Thank you for always being there and being more special than ever.

Stone and Debra Phillips, Dr. Thomas and Molly McWeeney, Gene and Cathy Tupper and John and Susi Whittaker for always listening and your love and support.

The Linda and John Daily family for allowing us to carry a golf bag in honor of Mark. It was truly a blessing and privilege for all.

My amazing college roommate, Marty Munson Zeller, who I miss every day and who continues to give me tons of strength.

Al and Lola McCloskey for your ongoing love and tremendous support over the years including helping make our Phoenix tournament such a big success.

George Fox University and the great privilege and honor to coach outstanding student-athletes. Additionally, President Robin Baker for his remarkable support, leadership and guidance. Also, to former President Dr. Dave Brandt for his belief in me.

The GFU Athletic Department who have given me and our teams great support over the years, including all those behind the scenes supporting us. Special shout-out to Patty Findley for all the airport shuttle rides for our team.

All our supporters, particularly Peggy and Bob Fowler, Brian Henninger, Stone and Debra Phillips, Dave, Pat and Jon Adrian, Keith Galitz, Gordon Crissman, Mike Delk, Dave and Betty DeHaven and John Kerekanich who have cheered on our teams and done so much for our GFU women's golf program!

All my mentors including coaches Linda Volstedt, Scott Rueck, Michael Meek, Paulette Pera, MaryLou Mulflur, Kailin Downs, Jodie Burton and friends and advisors Tresa Anderson, John Ducker, Mimi Nelson, Maureen Atchison, Ingrid Pentecost, and Laura Wozniak all who encouraged me to keep writing and to keep being me. Thanks for listening and all your great wisdom.

All the players I have coached. You have helped me learn and grow stronger than ever. Thank you for your willingness to work hard and all the inspiration.

Special note to our first team, Robin Taylor, Nicole Hudson Ernst,

Christine Collier Clair and Whitney Clunes Hartner for starting us off with amazing work ethic and championship gusto!

All the parents of players who I have had the honor to coach. Your contribution and love for our team is so appreciated.

All the coaches I have worked with and continue to work with today. You push me and make me better.

All the teammates and players I competed with over the years. Big thank you to Valerie DeVoe for your inspiration and to Ann O'Neil for keeping it fun. Also, to Soon Lee for teaching me the meaning of playing with "Joy" and "Zen" and to Dona Melrose for always making me laugh! Finally, to Shawn Hoffman for being there when I needed you.

My fellow classmates and teachers at St. Mary's Academy in Portland, Oregon, who inspired me, motivated me to work harder and achieve more. Very grateful for Varsity Basketball Coach Kathy Kinyon, who I had the opportunity to watch in action when I was the team basketball manager. Her passion as a female coach in a role dominated by men at the time had a big impact on me. And of course to my wonderful golf coach, Sister Jean Rose for all her wisdom and patience.

All the golf courses, club members and pros who have given our teams the privilege to use their practice facilities and courses including Chehalem Glenn GC, Willamette Valley CC and Langdon Farms GC. Special thank you to John Grothe, Head Golf Professional at Willamette Valley GC for his swing assistance with our teams over the years. Also, to Jason Burnett, our Master Club fitter at Redtail GC.

A special shout out to Westbrook Village Golf Club in Peoria, AZ for their support of our Westbrook Invitational over the years and Head Professional, Brandon Evans and all of his assistants who have helped with our event. Also, to our number one fan who is always there to support us, Matt Wilder.

The First Tee of Portland and Tournament Golf Foundation for all that you do for our community.

All my family (West and East Coasts!) friends and colleagues who have been there and enriched my life.

My amazing parents and grandparents who taught me that serving and loving others wholeheartedly is the ultimate reason we are here.

And finally, and most importantly, I want to express my deepest gratitude and glory to God, for all the guidance, grace and blessings I have received along my journey.

NOTES

1. I'VE GOT THE MUSIC IN ME

1. "History of Title IX." *Women's Sports Foundation*, 19 July 2021, www.womenssports-foundation.org/advocacy/history-of-title-ix.
2. *U.S. Department of Education*, 11 Dec. 1979, www2.ed.gov/about/of-fices/list/ocr/docs/t9interp.html,
3. "The Golf Channel." *U.S. Open Preview*, performance by Jaime Diaz, 13 June 2023.

2. WILL IT GO ROUND IN CIRCLES

1. "John McEnroe's Epic Wimbledon Meltdown: 'you Cannot Be Serious!' | ESPN Archives." *YouTube*, June 1981, www.youtube.com/watch?v=ransFQVzf6c%2C.
2. Young, Emma. "Lifting the Lid on the Unconscious." *New Scientist*, 26 July 2018, www.newscientist.com/article/mg23931880-400-lifting-the-lid-on-the-uncon scious/.
3. MOAWAD, TREVOR. *Getting to Neutral: How to Survive and Thrive in a Chaotic World.* HARPER ONE, 2022.

3. TURN THE BEAT AROUND

1. Janelle, Christopher M. "Ironic Mental Processes in Sport: Implications for Sport Psychologists." *Human Kinetics*, 1 June 1999, journals.humankinetics.com/view/journals/tsp/13/2/article-p201.xml.
2. Murphy, Joseph, and Arthur R. Pell. *The Power of Your Subconscious Mind.* Prentice Hall Press, 2008.
3. Hicks, Jerry, et al. *Ask and It Is Given: Learning to Manifest Your Desires.* Hay House, 2005.

4. ROCK THE BOAT, BABY!

1. Lrj. "5 Quotes by Serena Williams on Believing in Yourself." *The Leader Reader Journal*, 31 May 2020, leaderreaderjournal.com/5-quotes-by-serena-williams-on-believing-in-yourself/.
2. Godin, Seth. *Survival Is Not Enough: Why Smart Companies Abandon Worry and Embrace Change.* Free Press, 2002.

6. GOOD, GOOD, GOOD VIBRATIONS

1. Graham, Deborah, and Jon Stabler. *8 Traits of Champion Golfers: How to Develop the Mental Game of a Pro.* Simon & Schuster, 2001.
2. Pichardo, Gabriela. "What Is 4-7-8 Breathing? The Benefits of Mindful Breathing on Health and Wellness." *WebMD*, www.webmd.com/balance/what-to-know-4-7-8-breathing. Accessed 14 Aug. 2023.

7. GONNA FLY NOW

1. DeVries, Henry. "Managing Projects as a Boss as Seth Godin Does ." *Forbes*, June 2018.
2. Bernstein, Gabrielle. "How to Turn Dreams into Reality in 3 Steps." *Well+Good*, 7 Aug. 2020, www.wellandgood.com/gabby-bernstein-steps-to-achieve-dreams/.
3. Bell, Greg. *Water the Bamboo: 21 Strategies for Extraordinary Results in Your Profession or Team.* 2009.
4. Pressfield, Steven. *The War of Art: Break through the Blocks and Win Your Inner Creative Battles.* Black Irish Entertainment, LLC, 2012.

8. WALKING ON SUNSHINE—AND DON'T IT FEEL GOOD

1. Sarah Grynberg, *A Life of Greatness* podcast with Seth Godin on How to be your best self date? Grynberg, Sarah. "Sarah Grynberg, A Life of Greatness Podcast." *Seth Godin: How to Be Your Best Self,* season 4, episode 25, 2 Nov. 2020.

9. PICK UP THE PIECES

1. Suzuki, Shunryū, and Trudy Dixon. *Zen Mind, Beginner's Mind.* Shambhala, 2020.

10. SUPER TROUPER LIGHTS ARE GONNA FIND ME

1. Coyle, Daniel. *The Little Book of Talent: 52 Tips for Improving Skills.* Bantam Books, 2012.

11. TELL ME SOMETHING GOOD

1. "Dr. Bob Rotella." Women's Golf Coaches Assoc. and Golf Coaches Assn. of America Annual Coaches Convention. Dec. 2017, Las Vegas, NV, Planet Hollywood.
2. Heljala, Hannu. "How to Use the Power of the Subconscious Mind to Succeed." *Management 3.0,* 18 July 2022, management30.com/blog/subconscious-success/.
3. Korba, Rodney. *The Rate of Inner Speech - Rodney J. Korba, 1990 - Sage Journals,* journals.sagepub.com/doi/abs/10.2466/pms.1990.71.3.1043. Accessed 15 Aug. 2023.
4. Mylett, Ed. "Destroy Negative Thoughts with Trevor Moawad." *The Ed Mylett Show,* 12 May 2020.

5. Gordon, Jon. *The Carpenter: A Story about the Greatest Success Strategies of All.* John Wiley & Sons, Inc., 2014.

13. YOU GET WHAT YOU GIVE

1. Rotella, Bob. "Dr. Bob Rotella: Inside the Golfer's Mind." *Golf Digest,* www.golfdigest.com/story/rotella. Accessed 14 Aug. 2023.
2. Kerr-Dineen, Luke. "'Spot': How One Word Won Rory McIlroy the 2014 British Open." *GolfDigest.Com,* 14 July 2023, www.golfdigest.com/story/rory-mcilroy-2014-open-championship-putting-spot.

14. UNDER PRESSURE

1. Herman, Todd. *The Alter Ego Effect: The Power of Secret Identities to Transform Your Life.* Harper Business, an Imprint of HarperCollinsPublishers, 2019.
2. "Dr. David Cook." Women's Golf Coaches Assoc. and Golf Coaches Assn. of America Annual Coaches Convention. Dec. 2019, Las Vegas, NV, Planet Hollywood.

16. AIN'T NO MOUNTAIN HIGH ENOUGH

1. Itzler, Jesse. *Living with a Seal: 31 Days Training with the Toughest Man on the Planet.* Center Street, 2016.
2. SHARI, GROVER TIM S. WENK. *Winning: The Unforgiving Race to Greatness.* SIMON & SCHUSTER LTD, 2022.

17. I'VE GOT TO USE MY IMAGINATION

1. Godin, Seth. *This Is Marketing: You Can't Be Seen until You Learn to See.* Penguin Business, 2019.
2. Pressfield, Steven. *The War of Art: Break through the Blocks and Win Your Inner Creative Battles.* Black Irish Entertainment, LLC, 2012.
3. Jordan, Michael. "A Quote by Michael Jordan." *Goodreads,* www.goodreads.com/quotes/29242-obstacles-don-t-have-to-stop-you-if-you-run-into. Accessed 14 Aug. 2023.
4. Rotella, Bob. "Dr. Bob Rotella: Inside the Golfer's Mind." *Golf Digest,* www.golfdigest.com/story/rotella. Accessed 14 Aug. 2023.
5. Forleo, Marie. *Everything Is Figureoutable.* Penguin Putnam Inc, 2020.

18. BLANK SPACE

1. Grant, Ed. *Subconscious Golf.* CreateSpace Independent Publishing, 2013.
2. Max Homa, Golf Channel broadcast. date Max Homa, 2023. "'I Felt Free Today': Pressure off, Homa (62) Goes Low in Round 2." *Golf Channel,* Aug. 2022, www.golfchannel.com/news/i-felt-free-today-pressure-homa-62-goes-low-round-2.

19. I WILL SURVIVE

1. Cook, David Lamar. *Seven Days in Utopia: Golf's Sacred Journey.* Zondervan, 2011.

20. NOT ALL HEROES WEAR CAPES

1. Suzuki, Shunryū, and Trudy Dixon. *Zen Mind, Beginner's Mind.* Shambhala, 2020.
2. "Butch Harmon." Women's Golf Coaches Assoc. and Golf Coaches Assn. of America Annual Coaches Convention. Dec. 2015, Las Vegas, NV, Planet Hollywood.
3. Witherspoon, Reese. "Reese Witherspoon on Turning Impostor Syndrome into Confidence (Transcript)." *TED,* www.ted.com/podcasts/reese-witherspoon-on-impostor-syndrome-confidence-transcript. Accessed 14 Aug. 2023.

21. I JUST WANNA SHINE

1. Taylor, James. "Secret of Life - James Taylor." *YouTube,* 24 Nov. 2010.
2. "Ordinary People Do Extraordinary Things Every Day." *Jaburg Wilk,* 11 June 2019, www.jaburgwilk.com/news-publications/ordinary-people-do-extraordinary-things-every-day#:~:text=I%20first%20remember%20reading%20or,in%20the%20N-CAA%20Men's%20Basketball.

PERSPECTIVE

1. Clark, Wyndham. "'I Know She's Proud of Me' Wyndham Clark Pays Emotional Tribute to His Late Mother | golf | u.s. Open." *YouTube,* 18 June 2023, www.youtube.com/watch?v=GZbjDcxu5bk.

ABOUT THE AUTHOR

MaryJo McCloskey is a six-time NCAA Division-III West Region Coach of the Year and a nine-time Northwest Conference Coach of the Year. In 2006, Coach McCloskey launched the first George Fox University women's golf program and since then has led the team to prestige as one of the most dominant in the country with seven NCAA trophies including winning a National Championship and 11 consecutive top-10 finishes on the National stage.

The team has also won 13 straight Northwest Conference titles. To date, the program has won 97 tournaments and has been recognized in three separate seasons as the top-ranked team in the nation. The program also boasts a NCAA Individual National Champion, two NCAA Individual National Runner-Ups, two National Players of the Year, three NCAA Freshman Player of the Year honorees, 27 Women Golf Coaches Assn (WGCA) All Americans, 34 WGCA All-Region team members, 10 NWC Player of the Year honorees, 57 All-NW Conference players, and 24 WGCA All-American Scholar winners. Players from her program have qualified for the US Women's Amateur as well as for the LPGA Portland Classic event.

In 2013, Coach McCloskey was promoted to the role of Director of Golf for George Fox, one of the first women to be named to that position in NCAA Division-III and oversees the development of both the men's and women's golf teams at the university.

For Coach McCloskey, it's never been about awards but helping young women (and men) find their greatness. Her passion is to help student-athletes grow stronger and realize that anything is possible with a positive mindset, strong work ethic, and a passionate desire to learn.

McCloskey served 2 terms as D-III Director on the Board of Directors for the Women Golf Coaches Association (WGCA). She is currently serving on the NCAA Division-III Women's Golf Regional Championship Selection Committee and is also a part of the WGCA Mentorship program.

McCloskey has served on the Tournament Golf Foundation Board (operators of the LPGA Portland Classic) and many years on the First Tee of Portland/Campbell Course Board of Directors. She continues to help out as a volunteer for both organizations.

In 2023, Coach McCloskey was recognized by St. Mary's Academy in Portland, Oregon for Outstanding Achievement in Athletics and also nominated and placed on the ballot for the Oregon Sports Hall of Fame.

McCloskey holds Master of Business Administration (MBA) from the University of Portland and a Bachelor of Arts in Marketing from the University of Oregon.

www.ingramcontent.com/pod-product-compliance
Lightning Source LLC
Chambersburg PA
CBHW071153130626
46553CB00004B/1634